*California Natural History Guides: 14*

# NATIVE TREES

## OF

## SOUTHERN CALIFORNIA

BY

## P. VICTOR PETERSON

Illustrated by
Rita Whitmore

D0862116

UNIVERSITY OF CALIFORNIA PRESS
BERKELEY, LOS ANGELES, LONDON

UNIVERSITY OF CALIFORNIA PRESS
BERKELEY AND LOS ANGELES
UNIVERSITY OF CALIFORNIA PRESS, LTD.
LONDON, ENGLAND
© 1966 BY THE REGENTS OF THE UNIVERSITY OF CALIFORNIA

STANDARD BOOK NUMBER 520-01004-3
LIBRARY OF CONGRESS CATALOG NUMBER 65-26647
PRINTED IN THE UNITED STATES OF AMERICA

5 6 7 8 9 0

# CONTENTS

## INTRODUCTION

Trees, like individuals, become increasingly more interesting as we become better acquainted with them. As we travel about the state we are impressed with the great number of different trees which we encounter. On the high mountain trail they may be picturesque, wind-blown Western Junipers or the Limber Pines with their long and drooping branches. A little farther down the trail the Lodgepole Pine with its flaky bark and the white-trunked Quaking Aspen make their appearance. Still farther down the mountainside we meet the majestic Sugar Pine with long pendant cones hanging from the ends of its branches, the White Fir with erect cones glistening in the sunlight near the ends of its topmost branches, the Incense Cedar with its cinnamon-brown trunks, the lacy Douglas Fir, the Black Oak that was so important in the lives of the early Indians, and a host of other interesting trees.

Finally, as we approach the dry foothills, the Digger Pine with its forked trunk, long gray-green needles, and big cones tells us that we have reached the lower limits of the conifers. On the valley floors below the rolling foothills, we find an entirely new group of trees such as the characteristic Valley Oak, the Fremont Cottonwood, and many other broadleaf trees. As we approach the desert these trees tend to be replaced by the weird and grotesque Joshua Tree and the Yuccas which begin to dot the landscape.

An entirely different scene is found along the central coastal area where the sprawling, picturesque pines and cypresses of the Monterey Peninsula are silhouetted against the white sands and blue ocean, forming a series of never-to-be-forgotten vistas.

We are fortunate in California that so many areas have been set aside by the federal, state, or local governments to preserve for all time some of the beautiful and spectacular natural scenery with which we are so abundantly blessed.

Native trees are major attractions in such areas as Torrey Pine State Park, Pfeiffer Big Sur State Park, Point Lobos State Park, Anza-Borrego Desert State Park, Joshua Tree National Monument, and, in northern California, Sequoia National Park, Big Basin State Park, Muir Wood National Monument, and numerous state parks along the Redwood Highway from Armstrong Redwoods State Park near Santa Rosa to the Oregon border. It is with deep appreciation that we recognize the legislative foresight in establishing these areas to thrill and inspire mankind for generations to come. More should be established before it is too late.

Make it a habit as you travel the highways and byways of our state or as you camp on the banks of some stream or lake or in the shadow of the mountains, to become better acquainted with our beautiful native trees—you will find it rewarding. It is with this thought in mind that this volume has been prepared as a guide to aid in the recognition of the native trees of southern California, for only as you know them by name can you think or talk about them.

Southern California, for the purpose of this book, encompasses all of California from the Tehachapi Mountains south to the Mexican border, also including Santa Barbara, San Luis Obispo, and Monterey counties on the coast and Inyo County east of the Sierra Nevada. For trees north of Monterey Bay see *Native Trees of the San Francisco Bay Region* (University of California Press) by Woodbridge Metcalf.

Only trees native to the area are treated in this volume. To identify any of the hundreds of introduced species, a person should consult one of the more extensive publications dealing with cultivated trees. Nursery catalogs, nurserymen, teachers of botany or forestry, landscape designers, or the owners of particular trees may prove helpful in identifying an individual specimen. Many of our beautiful ornamental trees are either of foreign origin or may be the product of careful and scientific hybridizing. In many cases, the common names applied to these non-native hybridized trees bear no relationship to the names of their ancestors. Even though the great majority of our street and park trees are non-native, the charm and beauty of many of our native trees should not be overlooked when planning home or community grounds.

ACKNOWLEDGMENTS

I wish to express my sincere appreciation to the many people who have furnished information relative to the location of certain species of native trees described in this book, especially to Robert Beggs for his assistance in the San Jacinto Mountain area; to the rangers and naturalists of the various state parks of southern California; to Dr. Philip A. Munz, Director Emeritus of Rancho Santa Ana Botanic Garden; to Dr. Katherine Muller, Director of the Santa Barbara Botanic Garden; to the late Dr. Robert D. Rhodes, formerly Dean of Instruction, Long Beach State College; to Dr. Carl D. Duncan, Professor of Botany and Entomology, San Jose State College, and Mrs. Helen Sharsmith, Senior Herbarium Botanist, University Herbarium, University of California, Berkeley, who critically read the original manuscript and contributed many suggestions; to Dr. Lawrence Clark Powell and the University of California Library, Los Angeles, for permission to reproduce in reduced form the Eugene Murman watercolor drawings which are a part of a special collection of that library; and to the many others who have rendered valuable assistance.

# WHAT IS A TREE?

A tree, as defined in this book, is a woody plant at least ten feet high with a distinct stem or trunk not less than two inches in diameter and, except for unbranched yuccas or palms, with a more or less well-defined crown. Southern California shrubs are treated in *Native Shrubs of Southern California*, by Peter H. Raven, University of California Press. It is rather difficult to describe specifically the physical characteristics of all members even of a single species. The growth pattern of an individual specimen will, in many cases, depend markedly upon the surrounding conditions. One will frequently find certain oaks or willows that appear quite shrubby, while members of the same species growing under ideal conditions will develop into definitely tree-like specimens. Caution must also be exercised in comparing the size, shape, and characteristics of an individual leaf with the accepted standard. Averages should always be used when making comparisons. Fruit characteristics usually show less variation than leaves. Bark characteristics also are inconclusive. However, as one becomes familiar with the general characteristics, leaves, fruit, bark, and silhouette, the identification of individual species becomes less difficult and the effort more gratifying.

Leaves of trees may be classified as broad or narrow. Leaves that are generally three-sixteenths inch wide or less are, in this publication, classed as narrow leaves. They may be needle-shaped (pines), linear (firs), or scale-shaped (cypresses). Trees with such leaves are all evergreen since they retain their leaves

## A TREE IS A PLANT

with a trunk or stem

that is

woody

10 or more
feet high

2 or more inches
in diameter

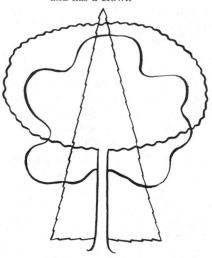

and has a crown

## A TREE HAS

leaves

a trunk

roots

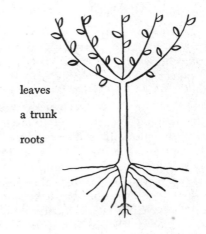

flowers and fruits

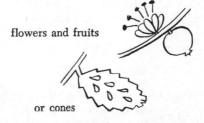

or cones

that produce seeds

for more than one season. Leaves that are generally more than three-sixteenths of an inch wide are classed as broad leaves. They may be either simple or compound, may have margins which smooth, toothed, serrated, or lobed, and may be arranged opposite each other or alternately along the stem. Trees with broad leaves may be either deciduous or evergreen.

## HOW TO IDENTIFY TREES

There are many features which contribute to the recognition of a particular species of tree, such as leaves, flowers, fruit, bark, size, silhouette, and habitat. However, leaves probably offer the best initial clue, since they are usually distinctive and in most cases may be found on the tree or the ground nearby. With this thought in mind, the following simple key has been prepared. In some cases the key leads directly to a specific tree, in other cases to groups of related trees. When the tree or group has been identified with the aid of the key, turn to the description in the text and to the illustration for further and final verification. If you have not used identification keys before see the section on the use of natural history keys in Jaeger and Smith, *Introduction to the Natural History of Southern California,* University of California Press.

1. Leaves generally less than 3/16 inch wide.*
                            The Conifers  P. 28
  A Leaves needle shaped and arranged in bundles of 1 to 5, each bundle wrapped at the base with a sheath of brownish, papery scales. ........................The Pines  P. 29
  B Leaves linear, more than ½ inch long. The false hemlocks, the firs, and Coast Redwood ........................ Pp. 42-46
  C Leaves scale shaped . . . Incense Cedar, the cypresses, and the junipers ........................................ P. 47
1. Leaves generally more than 3/16 inch wide.*
                        The Broadleaf Trees  P. 54

*Exception: leaves of Smoke Tree, few, 1/16 to ⅛ inch wide, ¼ to 1 inch long.

To distinguish between certain species of the same genus, one will frequently need to compare other features in addition to leaves, such as flowers, fruit, bark characteristics, size, silhouette, and habitat. The height indicated in the general description for each species applies to the mature tree in its natural habitat unless otherwise indicated. The dates listed in the text following the description of leaves, flowers, and fruit refer to the average flowering period of that species when it is found in its natural habitat.

## LEAVES

### ARE ON EVERGREEN TREES

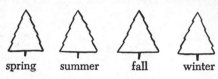

spring    summer    fall    winter

### OR ON DECIDUOUS TREES

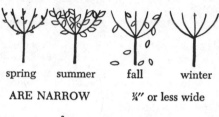

spring    summer    fall    winter

### ARE NARROW    ¼″ or less wide

### OR BROAD    more than ¼″ wide

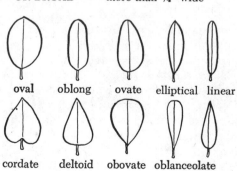

oval    oblong    ovate    elliptical    linear

cordate    deltoid    obovate    oblanceolate

lanceolate

[ 14 ]

LEAVES
ARE SIMPLE OR COMPOUND

ARE OPPOSITE OR ALTERNATE

Pinnate, bipinnate, tripinnate, or palmate

HAVE MARGINS THAT ARE

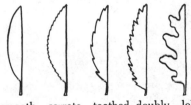

smooth   serrate   toothed   doubly   lobed
                              toothed

Digger Pine    Sugar Pine
  One Leaf Piñon Pine   Monterey Pine

### RECOGNIZING TREES AT A DISTANCE

After you become expert at identifying trees close up you may wish to develop your skill at telling them from afar. In most cases certain characteristics of the silhouette are sufficiently distinctive so that with practice the species may be identified as you drive by in your car. Verification by hiking over for a close look at the leaves will enable you to fix in mind the characteristics to watch for the next time you see the tree in question. To assist you in learning to recognize trees from a distance, some of the common trees are illustrated in silhouette and their characteristics are discussed. More and more of our attractive native trees are being planted in parks, along our city streets and in the gardens of many California homes far from their native habitat. Under these conditions their silhouettes may vary somewhat from those found undisturbed in nature.

Incense Cedar          Western Juniper
        Monterey Cypress                     White Fir

The Sugar Pine *(Pinus lambertiana)* is readily recognized by its long, pendulous cones which hang from
near the ends of the characteristic horizontal branches.

The Monterey Pine *(Pinus radiata)*, which is frequently windswept and somewhat open when found in
its native habitat near the coast, develops a rounder
and somewhat full silhouette in protected areas, or
even a pole-like form when found in thick stands. Its
persistent medium-sized closed or partially closed
cones which are found in whorls around the branches
and even around the trunks of younger trees become
an important factor in its identification. However, it
must not be confused with other native and non-
native pines which also produce persistent cones in
whorls. Its rich, deep green color will also prove
helpful in its identification.

The Digger Pine *(Pinus sabiniana)* is most readily
recognized by its long, gray-green needles, large cones,
and forked trunk. It must not be confused with the
Coulter Pine *(Pinus coulteri)*, which also produces

[ 17 ]

large, heavy cones, has a straight trunk and foliage which is dark green resembling somewhat the foliage of the Jeffrey Pine.

The One Leaf Piñon Pine *(Pinus monophylla)* is our only one-needle native pine. Young trees are quite pryramidal, but with age the lower branches die and the upper branches tend to spread, producing a somewhat more irregular and open crown. It is found primarily on dry slopes and frequently with the California Juniper *(Juniperus californica)*.

The young White Fir *(Abies concolor)* is a beautiful pyramidal tree; with age the crown tends to become roundish. Many old trees have dead and irregular tops. Cones of all firs stand erect on the topmost branches and disintegrate on the tree. Cones of the White Fir are somewhat smaller than those of the Red Fir *(Abies magnifica)*.

The young Incense Cedar *(Callocedrus decurrens)* is another beautiful pyramidal tree. Crowns of the older trees tend to become open and irregular. The flattened leaf-bearing twigs which lie primarily in one plane tend to give the tree a somewhat lacy appearance. Its trunk and thick fibrous cinnamon-brown bark resemble somewhat the trunk and bark of the Giant Sequoia *(Sequoia gigantea)*.

The wind-blown mature Monterey Cypress *(Cupressus macrocarpa)* is one of our most picturesque coastal trees. Young and protected trees are usually sharply conical: however, with exposure and maturity, they tend to develop a wide, flat top and umbrella-shaped crown.

A mature Western Juniper *(Juniperus occidentalis)*, the picturesque monarch of the high mountains, is readily recognized by its usually gnarled form, short, stocky, weather-beaten, cinnamon-brown tapering trunk, and its flat top and open crown. However, in a more favorable environment, it frequently develops a straight and less tapering trunk and a somewhat

Coast Redwood

pyramidal crown. The bark on more protected trees is usually less fluted and not as deeply colored as that of the older trees found in a more severe environment.

The Coast Redwood *(Sequoia sempervirens)* is our tallest, largest, and most spectacular coastal tree, attaining a height in northern California of over 350 feet. Old trees have large columnar branchless trunks with thick fibrous reddish-brown fissured bark. The pyramidal crowns of young trees tend to become rounded, sometimes open, and nearly flat in old trees.

The Black Cottonwood *(Populus trichocarpa)* is frequently found along stream beds or in damp places. It is a large deciduous tree with spreading branches tending to form a broad, open, roundish crown. Trunks of mature trees are usually branchless for some distance. Leaves are dark-green above, giving the tree a somewhat dark appearance. Leaves tend to turn yellow in the autumn. It must not be confused with the somewhat smaller Fremont Cottonwood *(Populus fremontii)* whose leaves are yellowish-green above and, although they have a flattened leaf stalk, do not flutter so obviously as do the leaves of the Aspen.

The Aspen *(Populus tremuloides)* is one of our most colorful high-mountain trees. It is a slender tree irregularly branched and usually found in close stands on slopes and mountain flats. Its green-white trunks with dull-green summer leaves that turn yellow in the autumn create a spectacular vista. Its flattened leaf stalks cause the leaves to flutter in the breeze, a readily recognizable characteristic of the Aspen.

The individual species of willows are rather difficult to identify by silhouette alone; however, the members of the Willow family are readily recognized by their shape and habitat. They are most frequently found along stream banks and in moist places from sea level to the high mountains. Some of the numerous species found in California are quite shrub-like while others develop into sizable trees. Many species have a profusion of whip-like branches. Most species have leaves which are long and narrow.

The Red Willow *(Salix laevigata)*, although occasionally somewhat shrubby, generally assumes tree-like proportions. Its trunk is usually somewhat branched,

Black Cottonwood     Sandbar Willow
       Aspen             Red Willow

however, it will commonly have one main trunk. Its branches form a somewhat irregular crown.

The Sandbar Willow *(Salix hindsiana)* is a small tree, frequently quite shrubby. It occurs usually along open ditches, on sand bars or flood beds.

The Coast Live Oak *(Quercus agrifolia)* is the most common broadleaf evergreen tree of the California coastal foothills and valleys. Young trees tend to have a full and rounded crown. With age, however, some major branches tend to spread and produce a broad, irregular, and open crown. This tendency to spread is in contrast to the behavior of the Interior Live Oak *(Quercus wislizeni)*, which generally maintains a more compact and rounded crown throughout its life.

The Valley Oak *(Quercus lobata)* is the monarch of all California deciduous oaks. It is found throughout the central valleys and into the foothills. Its form varies greatly from tall, erect trees with rather sparse crowns and short outer drooping branches to those

Coast Live Oak                California Black Oak
Valley Oak

with wide-spreading branches and rather full crowns. The bark of the mature tree is usually thick, dark gray, and checkered.

The California Black Oak *(Quercus kelloggii)* is another spectacular deciduous oak which undoubtedly derived its name because of its very dark-colored bark. Leaves when first appearing on young shoots in the early spring may be bright pink to crimson. All leaves become shiny bright green as they mature and usually turn yellow to reddish in the fall, producing an interesting color effect on the California foothills and mountains. At lower elevations it is a graceful tree with a broad, rounded crown while at higher elevations it tends to be somewhat more irregularly branched and may, on occasion, develop an almost prostrate form.

The Big Leaf Maple *(Acer macrophyllum)* has a broad and rounded crown when found in the open, although usually not as compact as many introduced species. Under crowded conditions it may become

Big Leaf Maple                    Western Sycamore
                White Alder

quite rangy and ragged. Its dark green deeply-lobed
leaves vary greatly in size. In deep shade some may
be twelve or more inches wide, while in open sun
some may be only about half that wide.

The Box Elder *(Acer negundo)*, when found in the
open, is a medium-sized tree, usually with a short
trunk and a broad, roundish crown, while in close
stands it tends to become somewhat pole-like and
open. Its leaves are pinnately compound in contrast
to the simple leaves of the other native maples.

The White Alder *(Alnus rhombifolia)* is found along
inland or mountain streams. It is readily recognized as
a graceful tree with a clear and usually straight trunk,
and open, spreading branches forming an oval crown.
Its whitish- or grayish-brown bark is broken into irregular plates on old trees. Alders produce small
woody cones. Careful observation is necessary to distinguish between the White and Red Alder *(Alnus
oregona)*.

The Western Sycamore *(Platanus racemosa)* is an-

[ 23 ]

Box Elder                    Western Redbud

other of the more conspicuous native California trees
and is usually found along old stream bottoms, banks
of running streams, and canyons. Sycamores vary in
from from tall, erect trees with heavy trunks to ones
with large, crooked trunks and branches which nearly
touch the ground. Bark on the lower trunks of old trees
is thick, dark brown, and furrowed: on upper trunks
and branches it is ashy-white and flaky, showing
mottled colors of gray, brown, and yellowish- and dull-
green. Leaves are pale green, large, and conspicuous.

The Madrone *(Arbutus menziesii)* is a handsome,
much-branched broadleaf evergreen tree. It is easily
recognized by its polished terra-cotta-colored bark
which usually appears under dark brown and scaling
older bark and by its dark, glossy green leaves, white
flowers, and brilliant orange-red berry-like fruit.

The California Buckeye *(Aesculus californica)* is a
small, compact tree which dots many of the dry slopes
of our California mountains and foothills. The trees
look like small green mounds on the hillsides shortly
after the first winter rains; in the spring or early sum-

Madrone    California Buckeye    California Laurel

mer they are literally covered with clusters of white flowers, but by midsummer the leaves turn brown, producing yet a different hillside effect. By late summer or early fall the leaves have all dropped, leaving conspicuous pear-shaped pods hanging from the ends of its branches.

The California Laurel *(Umbellularia californica)* is an interesting broadleaf evergreen tree which, when found in the open, produces a broad, rounded to modified pyramidal crown. When crowded it may develop a somewhat more open and irregular crown. In dry places, it may appear widely branched and somewhat shrubby. Its leaves have a distinctive green color which can readily be recognized at a distance.

The Western Redbud *(Cercis occidentalis)* is a small tree with a rounded crown that nearly reaches the ground. Its striking reddish-purple pea-like flowers which appear before the leaves make it one of our most attractive flowering trees.

The Honey Mesquite *(Prosopis glandulosa)* is a small desert tree with many crooked branches and a short trunk. It also occurs as a bushy shrub. Its small compound leaves produce a lacy effect.

The Palo Verde *(Cercidium floridum)* is another interesting desert tree. It is leafless for most of the year. The bark on young trunks and limbs is light yellowish- to bluish-green. On the trunks of mature trees it is light brown with a reddish tinge. It produces large seed pods which mature in mid-summer.

The mature California Fan Palm *(Washingtonia filifera)* is a tall, robust, columnar, unbranched tree with large, spreading fan-like leaves. Dead leaves droop and adhere close to the trunk of the trees for many years, causing the native undisturbed specimen to appear unkempt in contrast to the carefully pruned specimen found in parks, gardens, or parkways. It is the only native palm found in California. It has been extensively planted in many localities, hence care must be taken not to confuse it with some of the numerous domestic species which are so widely planted in the southland.

Palo Verde          Honey Mesquite

Mojave Yucca                    California Fan Palm
                    Joshua Tree

The Joshua Tree *(Yucca brevifolia)* is without doubt one of our most weird and unusual appearing desert trees. Young trees are without branches while older trees are much branched, producing a widespread and open crown. Its long (seven-to-twelve-inch), narrow, sharp, smooth, pale green leaves are clustered at the ends of the branches. Greenish-white flowers occur in dense compound clusters.

The Mojave Yucca *(Yucca schidigera)* is another strange desert tree, usually with a single unbranched trunk and with long, one-to-three foot, narrow, sharp leaves protruding in all directions. Its conspicuous creamy-white flowers are borne in a single, large, erect cluster.

# CONIFEROUS TREES

The conifers treated in this volume are all narrow-leaf evergreen trees and include the pines, firs, false hemlocks, redwood, cedar, cypresses, and junipers. Many species within these groups, such as the Coast Redwood, Douglas Fir, Western Yellow Pine, and Sugar Pine, are extremely important lumber trees. Less important, but of considerable commercial value, are the Jeffrey Pine, Lodgepole Pine, White Fir, and Incense Cedar. Other conifers are used for fuel, posts, pulp, and shoring. The lumber produced from conifers is relatively soft, strong, and light. It seasons well and works easily, making it by far the most important of all commercial woods. In view of its tremendous economic importance, large private lumber industries on the Pacific Coast are now actively engaged in an extensive reforestation program. The government is likewise concerned with controlled cutting in the National Forests, and in their reforestation. These practices will go far toward insuring a perpetual supply of this important commodity, as well as providing extensive recreational and limited grazing areas.

In addition to their economic value, many conifers find extensive use as ornamental trees.

Much of the forest area on the Pacific Coast is relatively marginal agricultural land. However, it will produce forest trees and it is therefore important that the best forest practices be established and maintained.

The fruit of all conifers described in this volume, except that of the junipers, are woody cones. The junipers produce a berry-like fruit, which, although not woody, is morphologically a cone. The size and characteristics of all cones described are those of the ripe cone.

## PINE FAMILY (PINACEAE)

The Pine family includes more members than any other family of native cone-bearing trees in California. The members (genera) of this large family included in this book are pines *(Pinus)*, false hemlock *(Pseudotsuga)*, and firs *(Abies)*.

### PINES (PINUS)

There are seventeen different species of native pines growing in the area included in this book: some are rare and geographically quite restricted, others are common and widespread. Some, such as the Western Yellow Pine and the Sugar Pine, are important lumber trees, while others have little commercial value. Pines are distinguished from other members of the family by the fact that their needle-like leaves occur in bundles of one to five enclosed at the base by a sheath of papery scales. Cones ripen during the second or third season.

For the purpose of identification we will divide the pines into groups based on the number of leaves in a bundle, and henceforth, will refer to these leaves as needles.

### One-Needle Pines

**One Leaf Pinon Pine** *(Pinus monophylla)*

This pine is commonly known as one of the nut pines since its seeds are large and edible. The nuts were extensively gathered by Indians who lived in the area and used them as an important item of food. The cones, when mature, open and disperse their seeds over some little distance, which made gathering the crop a rather tedious task. Moreover, when the seeds were thus scattered, keen-eyed birds, squirrels, and other animals were quick to discover their presence, much to the disgust of the Indians. However, they eventually learned that if the cones were gathered just before they were ripe, dried, and then placed around a fire, they would open and release their seeds. They also discovered that the heat made the seeds more palatable and that it was a great deal easier to gather the seeds from around the fire than from the grass in competition with the birds and squirrels.

The Piñon Pine is an extremely slow-growing, small and symmetrical tree, usually not more than 30 feet tall; many trees reach an age of over two hundred years. In recent years Piñon Pines have been extensively harvested as Christmas trees. Residential subdivisions are also making inroads into its natural habitats. Unless these practices are controlled, we will soon find this beautiful little tree reaching a point of extinction. To forestall such a catastrophe, efforts should be initiated to have certain remaining undisturbed areas set aside as public reservations.

*Leaves and fruit:* Needles usually in ones, 1 to 2 in. long, stiff, and slightly curved towards the stem. The cones mature in August of the second growing season. Seeds are dark chocolate-brown and about ½ in. long.

*Range:* Arid slopes of the mountains in southeastern California, on the eastern slopes of the Sierra Nevada, and sparsely in the mountains of San Bernardino, Ventura, Los Angeles, Riverside, and San Diego counties. Frequently found with the California Juniper, rarely cultivated. May. Piñon—Juniper Woodland.

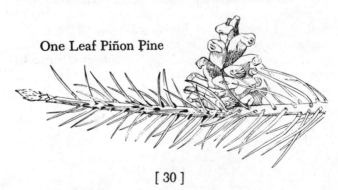

One Leaf Piñon Pine

## Two-Needle Pines

**Lodgepole Pine** *(Pinus murrayana)*

Also known as Tamarack Pine, this is a tall and slender tree when found in dense stands, heavier and branched in open stands, 50 to 100 ft. tall. Its bark is thin and covered with small scales. The wood is light, soft, and straight-grained and is used extensively for poles, railroad ties, mine timbers, box shooks, laths, and pulp. Fire and pine beetle cause heavy losses annually. It is rarely seen in cultivation. Cones, either as they are naturally or sprayed with silver or gold paint, make attractive Christmas decorations.

*Leaves and fruit:* Yellow green needles in twos, 1 to 2½ in. long and stiff. Cones 1 to 2 in. long, abundant; cone scales tipped with short, slender prickles.

*Range:* Widespread in borders of high mountain meadow and moist slopes from San Jacinto Mountains to Alaska. Found in the San Jacinto and San Bernardino Mountains at elevations of 7,000 to 10,000 ft. July. Lodgepole Pine—White Fir Forest.

**Bishop Pine** *(Pinus muricata)*

Mature trees in close stands may be quite slender and 50 to 75 ft. tall, while in open stands they may have densely pyramidal, rounded, or even flat crowns. It is frequently planted as a windbreak and occasionally as a park tree. The wood is strong, hard, and coarse-grained, and sometimes used for lumber. Unopened or partially opened cones will completely open in case of a fire and scatter their seeds, which, if the fire is not too intense, will germinate and produce a new stand of trees. Several other pines with similar characteristics such as the Monterey Pine, Knobcone Pine, and Santa Cruz Island Pine are discussed later. Closed cones may be artificially opened by placing them near an open fire or on a pan in a moderately hot oven.

*Leaves and fruit:* Dark yellow-green needles in twos or threes, 3½ to 5½ in. long. Cones 2 to 3½ in. long, borne in whorls of three to five frequently remaining closed or partially closed on the tree for many years.

*Range:* Scattered stands in the humid coastal region from Humboldt to Santa Barbara counties, on Huckleberry Hill in Monterey County, and on Santa Cruz Island. March-April. Closed-cone Pine Forest.

### Santa Cruz Island Pine *(Pinus remorata)*

This pine is a slender, medium-sized tree 30 to 50 ft. tall, with an open crown which tends to become flat-topped with age. It is quite similar to the Bishop Pine. H. L. Mason has stated that this species has been distinct since early Pleistocene and can be considered a remnant of a past flora.

*Leaves and fruit:* Dark green needles in twos, 3 to 8 in. long, rather stiff and twisted. Cones 2 to 3½ in. long, dark brown, sessile or very short-stalked, and extending straight out from the branches.

*Range:* Found near the La Purisima Mission in Santa Barbara County and on Santa Cruz Island where it is associated with the Bishop Pine. March—April. Closed-cone Pine Forest.

### Nut Pine *(Pinus edulis)*

This is a small handsome tree, 20 to 40 ft. tall.

*Leaves and fruit:* Dark green needles in twos, occasionally in threes on same tree, 1 to 2 in. long, stiff, sharp-pointed. Cones 1 to 2 in. long, seeds, about ½ in. long, are sold in markets as pine nuts.

*Range:* Little San Bernardino and New York Mountains, and also farther east in Arizona, New Mexico, and Texas. Sometimes associated with One Leaf Piñon Pine and California Juniper. Piñon—Juniper Woodland, Foothill Woodland.

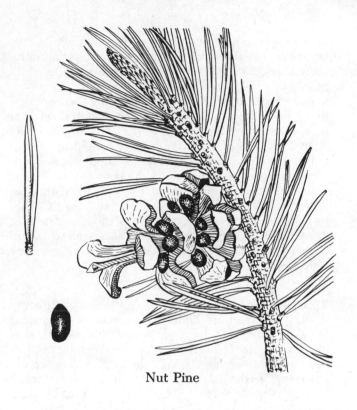

Nut Pine

## Three-Needle Pines

**Western Yellow Pine** *(Pinus ponderosa)*

The Western Yellow Pine, also known as Ponderosa Pine, is one of our most important lumber trees. Mature specimens vary greatly in size and appearance due to variations in soil and climatic conditions. Under ideal conditions some trees may attain a height of 200 ft. and a diameter of 5 to 6 ft. Under less favorable conditions, a height of only 70 to 80 ft. and a diameter of 16 to 20 in. may be its limit. Bark characteristics also vary greatly from large tawny-yellow or russet-brown platelets to hard, dark, and deeply furrowed

[ 33 ]

ridges on young trees or trees growing under less favorable conditions. Specimens showing the latter bark characteristics are frequently known as "bull pine."

*Leaves and fruit:* Yellow-green needles in threes, 5 to 10 in. long and densely clustered at the ends of branches. Cones 2 to 5 in. long, quite symmetrical, open, light-weight. Scales of mature cones tipped with out-turned pin-point prickles, pricking one's hands when they are cupped around the cone.

*Range:* Widespread throughout mountain areas at elevations of 1,000 to 9,000 ft. from San Diego County to British Columbia. Usually the predominant tree in areas where it occurs. Not plentiful in coastal mountains of southern California. May–June. Yellow Pine Forest.

### Jeffrey Pine *(Pinus jeffreyi)*

This pine, 60 to 180 ft. tall, is quite similar in many respects to Western Yellow Pine, and is considered by some authors to be a variety of this species. It is also known to hybridize with the Western Yellow Pine. There are, however, sufficient differences—cones, silhouette, bark, and habitat—to justify two distinct species. The bark of mature trees is usually dark reddish-brown and broken into irregular scaly plates. The deep furrows in the bark, when warmed in the sun, emit a pineapple- or vanilla-scented odor. Western Yellow Pine emits no such odor. Crowns tend to be longer and more symmetrical than those of the Yellow Pine. Lumber is quite similar to that of Yellow Pine.

*Leaves and fruit:* Blue-green needles in threes, 5 to 10 in. long. Foliage tends to be heavier and more dense than that of the Yellow Pine. Cones 5 to 10 in. long, proportionately heavier and bulkier than those of the Yellow Pine. Prickles on ends of mature cone scales are slightly incurved and usually do not prick hands when they are cupped around ripe cones.

[ 34 ]

*Range:* Widespread in the White Fir Forests from northern Baja California to southern Oregon. Found in the San Bernardino and San Jacinto Mountains at elevations of 5,000 to 9,500 ft. May—June. Lodgepole Pine—White Fir Forest, Yellow Pine Forest.

**Digger Pine** *(Pinus sabiniana)*

The Digger Pine, 50 to 70 ft. tall, is the first native conifer than one sees when entering the hot dry foothills of the Coast Ranges from the Santa Lucia Mountains to northern Los Angeles County. It is readily identified by its characteristic grey-green needles, large cones, and forked trunk. It owes its common name to the fact that its large seeds were an important item of food for the California Digger Indians. The wood is coarse-grained and has no real lumber value, but is used for fuel.

*Leaves and fruit:* Gray-green needles in threes, 7 to 13 in. long and usually drooping from the ends of the branches. Light brown cones 6 to 10 in. long and sometimes almost as broad. Cone scales end in a sharp, often hook-like spur. Cones may remain on the tree for several seasons after the seeds have been shed.

*Range:* Dry foothills bordering the central valleys and the inner Coast Range. In southern California from the Santa Lucia Mountains to northern Los Angeles County, also in the Tehachapi Pass. April—May. Southern Oak Woodland.

**Coulter Pine** *(Pinus coulteri)*

Also known as Big Cone Pine, this is a medium-sized tree, 40 to 80 ft. tall, with dark brown to nearly black bark. It is another of our interesting hot dry foothill conifers. Its cones resemble somewhat those of the Digger Pine, although larger. Its needles are similar in color to those of the Jeffrey Pine, but much longer. Wood is light, soft, and brittle. It is used as second-class lumber. Seeds were used by the Indians as food.

*Leaves and fruit:* Dark green needles in threes, 5 to 12 in. long, stiff, and sharp-pointed. Cones are yellowish brown, 9 to 14 in. long, the largest and heaviest produced by any native conifer. Cone scales have long, stout, incurved flattened spurs. Cones may stay on the tree for several years after shedding their seeds.

*Range:* Restricted to California. Found in the dry foothills of the San Bernardino, San Jacinto, and Cuyamaca Mountains at elevations of 1,000 to 7,000 ft., and in the inner Coastal Range as far north as Contra Costa County. May—June. Southern Oak Woodland, Yellow Pine Forest.

### Monterey Pine  *(Pinus radiata)*

In protected areas, this picturesque pine will develop into a beautiful symmetrical tree 40 to 100 ft. tall. However, along the windswept coastal area it frequently assumes picturesque and grotesque shapes. In thick stands it develops a straight pole-like form. It is extensively planted in Australia, New Zealand, South America, Africa, and parts of Europe as a lumber tree.

*Leaves and fruit:* Rich green needles in threes, rarely in twos, 3 to 5 in. long. Cones 3 to 5 in. long, unsymmetrical, usually borne in whorls of 3 to 5, remain on the tree partially opened for many years. Cone scales on the outer side near the base have a rounded apex.

*Range:* Coastal area of Monterey County, near Monterey, Pacific Grove, Carmel, and in Point Lobos State Park, in San Luis Obispo County near Cambria and San Simeon, and in the coastal areas in Santa Cruz County. April. Closed-cone Pine Forest.

### Knobcone Pine  *(Pinus attenuata)*

A small, slender tree, 20 to 50 ft. tall, which usually has an open, rounded top, this is one of our most unusual trees from the standpoint of survival. Its cones, which adhere to the trunk or branches indefinitely, rarely open except in case of fire. Here, then, is a tree which depends almost entirely on a major catastrophe for its propagation. It is a spectacular sight to visit a Knobcone Pine forest which has recently been ravished by a fire and see the hundreds of cones on each tree popped wide open. If the fire were fast moving and not too hot, many of the seeds that had been released would germinate and produce trees to wait for the next fire. The wood is light, soft, and coarse grained.

*Leaves and fruit:* Pale yellow-green slender needles in threes, 3 to 5 in. long. Unsymmetrical cones 4 to 6 in. long and in whorls. Cone scales on the outer side and near the base have a pyramidal apex which is armed with a prickle.

*Range:* Widely scattered localities on the dry and rocky foothill slopes from southern Oregon to southern California. Found in the San Bernardino, San Jacinto, Santa Ana, and Santa Lucia Mountains. March—May. Closed-cone Pine Forest.


### Four-Needle Pine

**Parry Pine** *(Pinus quadrifolia)*

This is a short-trunked tree 15 to 30 feet tall, quite similar in growth habits to the One Leaf Piñon Pine. It is the only four-needle pine that is native to California. Its seeds were widely used as food by Indians in the early days.

*Leaves and fruit:* Needles pale green on top, whitish on under surface, mostly in fours, sometimes in threes or fives on the same tree, 1 to 1½ in. long, stiff, and incurved. Cones 1½ to 2 in. long.

*Range:* Scattered localities on dry slopes bordering the Colorado Desert, and from the Santa Rosa and San Jacinto Mountains to Lower California. May. Piñon—Juniper Woodland.

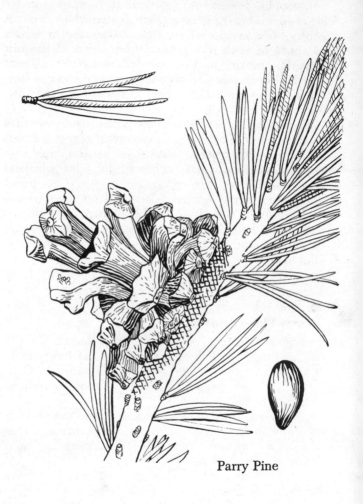

Parry Pine

## Five-Needle Pines

**Sugar Pine** *(Pinus lambertiana)*

The Sugar Pine is the largest of all native pines. A mature tree may reach a height of over 200 ft. and a diameter of 6 to 7 ft. In the southern part of its range it is somewhat smaller. It is one of our most magnificent cone-bearing trees and also the one which is the most easily recognized. The trunks of the mature trees are straight and only slightly tapering until its long, horizontal branches, which tend to form a flat crown, are reached. Young trees are gracefully symmetrical. Its large cones, either single, in twos, or occasionally in threes, hang pendent from the ends of the branches and serve to identify the tree from long distances. Cones ripen during the late summer of the second season, shed their seeds in the late fall, and usually drop during the late winter, spring, or early summer of the third season. The bark or mature trees is reddish-brown to purplish-grey, deeply furrowed, and with the ridges broken into irregular scaly plates; bark of young trees is dark grey and smooth. Wood is light, soft, straight-grained, and relatively free of knots. It is extensively used where a wood of its superior quality is required and consequently it commands a correspondingly high price. Prudent harvesting and utilization must be exercised in order to extend as long as possible the availability of this very desirable type wood. Unfortunately, it is disappearing faster than it is being replenished by even our most modern conservation techniques.

*Leaves and fruit:* Blue-green needles in fives, 3 to 4 in. long, usually sharp-pointed and clustered tassel-like at end of branches. Cones 12 to 20 in. long and 4 to 5 in. in diameter.

*Range:* Yellow Pine forests from Oregon to Baja California at elevations of 2,000 to 7,500 ft., higher in southern mountains. Scattered stands in Santa Barbara and Cuyamaca Mountains. Western limit follows in general the inland margin of fog belt, 20 to 30 miles from the coast. May–June. Yellow Pine Forest, Lodgepole Pine–White Fir Forest.

### Bristlecone Pine *(Pinus aristata)*

Also known as Hickory Pine, this is a medium-sized tree, 20 to 50 ft. tall, sometimes with a short, thick trunk. Its deep green foliage which is clustered near the ends of the branches tends to give the tree a bushy appearance. Bark on old trunks is dull reddish-brown, on young trunks and branches smooth and whitish. It is another of our interesting high mountain pines. Until 1956 the Sequoias were considered to be our oldest living trees, but then 4,000-year-old Bristlecone Pines were found in the White Mountains with cores of some specimens showing an age of 4,600 years.

*Leaves and fruit:* Dark green needles in fives, 1 to 1½ in. long, lustrous on upper and whitish on under surface. Ovoid cones purplish-brown, nearly sessile, 2½ to 3½ in. long. Cone scales thickened at apex and armed with a fragile uncurved prickle.

*Range:* Dry rocky slopes of Inyo, Panamint, and White Mountains at elevations of 7,500 to 11,500 ft., and east to Colorado. June–July. Bristlecone Pine Forest.

### Limber Pine *(Pinus flexilis)*

This is a low, thick-trunked, and much-branched tree, 25 to 50 ft. tall. Its crown consists of long drooping branches, in the case of young trees sometimes nearly reaching the ground. Branchlets are pliable and tough, which undoubtedly accounts for its name. Bark on mature trees is blackish or dark brown, on young trees whitish-gray. It is one of the less well-known pines, due doubtless to its high, relatively inaccessible range.

*Leaves and fruit:* Dark green needles in fives, 1½ to 3 in. long, stiff, and clustered tassel-like at the ends of the branches, cones 3 to 8 in. long. Tips of cone scales greatly thickened and often curved.

[ 40 ]

*Range:* Subalpine forests, eastern slope of the Sierra at elevations of 7,000 to 10,000 ft., Mt. Pinos at 8,500 to 8,800 ft., San Bernardino and San Jacinto Mountains at 9,000 to 11,500 ft. July—August. Lodgepole Pine—White Fir Forest.

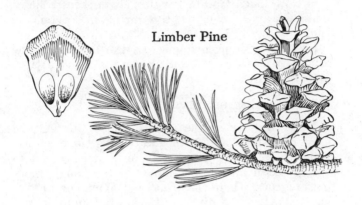

Limber Pine

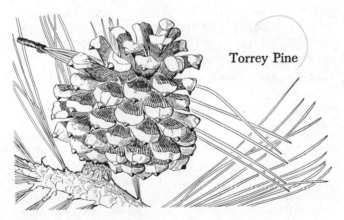

Torrey Pine

**Torrey Pine** *(Pinus torreyana)*

This is a sprawling tree, 20 to 40 ft. tall when exposed to strong sea winds. Away from the sea, it has a straight trunk and may reach a height of 50 to 60 ft. Geographically it is our most restricted native. Torrey Pine

[ 41 ]

State Park at the northern city limits of San Diego was established to preserve this unusual and picturesque pine.

*Leaves and fruit:* Dark green leaves in fives, 7 to 12 in. long, clustered at the ends of stout branches. Cones 4 to 6 in. long. Tips of cone scales thickened into a triangular apex, lower scales terminate in a pyramidal knob.

*Range:* Dry slopes below 500 ft. near Del Mar on the San Diego County coast and also on Santa Rosa Island. January–March.

### FALSE HEMLOCK (PSEUDOTSUGA)

There are two native false hemlocks in southern California, the Douglas Fir and the Big Cone Spruce. Young trees, when growing in open stands, tend to form graceful pyramidal silhouettes with long, drooping branches. Their flat, soft, and abundant needle-like leaves tend to give the trees a full and lacy appearance. The needles spiral completely around the twig, but usually appear two-ranked, due to very short twisted green petioles. Cones mature in one season.

**Douglas Fir** *(Pseudotsuga menziesii)*
This is a large forest tree 150 to 300 ft. tall, often with a massive clear trunk up to 100 feet or more. Douglas Firs in the southern part of their range are somewhat smaller. The typical pyramidal crown of a young tree with its horizontal and sometimes drooping branches tends to become rounded or somewhat flattened with maturity or in thick stands. Bark of mature trees is dark, furrowed, thick, and corky. Bark of young trees is smooth and grayish. It is our most important lumber tree and is commonly known in the trade as Oregon Pine, an erroneous name reputedly attributed to early midwestern lumbermen who came from an area where fir was a decidedly inferior lumber tree. Small trees

[ 42 ]

are used extensively as Christmas trees and widely planted as ornamentals.

*Leaves and fruit:* Leaves ¾ to 1½ in. long and about 1/16 in. wide, flat, blunt, blue-green on top, with two grayish bands beneath and very short twisted petioles. Leaves persist for 8 to 10 years. Cones 2 to 4 in. long, numerous, pendulous, and with conspicuous three-pointed bracts protruding between the cone scales.

*Range:* Coast Ranges, British Columbia to northern Santa Barbara County from sea level to 4,000 ft. and in the Sierra from Fresno County north at elevations of 2,500 to 6,000 ft. Yellow Pine Forest, Douglas Fir Forest, Broadleaf Evergreen Forest.

## Big Cone Spruce *(Pseudotsuga macrocarpa)*

This is a small to medium-sized tree 30 to 60 ft. tall. Its wide and pyramidal crown is open and thin. Lower branches are long, horizontal, and drooping. Bark of mature trees is blackish or deep reddish-brown. In some respects it is quite similar to the Douglas Fir. The wood does not make high-grade lumber.

*Leaves and fruit:* Cones similar to those of Douglas Fir but larger—4 to 7 in.—with the bracts only slightly protruding.

*Range:* Dry slopes and canyons from Santa Inez Mountains south to the Cuyamaca Mountains in San Diego County at elevations of 2,000 to 6,000 ft. Yellow Pine Forest, Chaparral.

FIRS (ABIES)

There are only two native firs in southern California, the White Fir and the Santa Lucia Fir. Firs are tall evergreen trees with characteristic conical crowns. Young trees when not crowded are beautifully symmetrical. Branches grow in whorls at regular intervals around the trunk. The erect cones are borne near the ends of the upper branches, mature in one season, and distintegrate on the trees. Firs are extensively sold as Christmas trees. Christmas tree farms are beginning to appear in the state and should be encouraged to reduce the indiscriminate cutting of young native trees. Firs produce lumber of varying quality and are considered important forest trees.

### White Fir *(Abies concolor)*

White Firs are tall, large forest trees 60 to 200 ft. tall. The crowns of mature trees tend to be roundish while those of young trees are pyramidal. Bark on the trunk of mature trees is deeply furrowed and ash-gray. Bark on upper branches and on young trees is smooth and grayish. It is frequently sold on the Christmas tree market under the erroneous name of "Silvertip." The wood is light, soft, and rather coarse-grained. It is used extensively as dimension lumber and as box wood. It tends to punk when exposed to excessive moisture. The twist at the base of the leaf serves with other characteristics to distinguish it from the Red Fir or true "Silvertip" whose leaves have no twist at their base. It is extensively planted as an ornamental.

*Leaves and fruit:* Leaves 1 to 2 in. long Leaves on lower branches longer than those on upper branches, about ⅛ in. wide, may be pointed, rounded, or slightly notched at apex, bluish-green, two whitish brands on under surface separated by greenish keel, twisted base causing leaves to appear two-ranked. Cones 2 to 5 in. high, erect on ends of upper branches.

*Range:* San Bernadino, San Jacinto, and Cuyamaca Mountains. May—June. Yellow Pine Forest, Lodgepole Pine—White Fir Forest.

### Santa Lucia Fir *(Abies bracteata)*

Also known as Bristlecone Fir, this is another rare, geographically restricted, and little-known tree, 30 to 100 ft. tall. Its sharp-pointed crown and lustrous green foliage make it readily recognized among its natural associates. It is occasionally cultivated due to its attractive foliage.

*Leaves and fruit:* Leaves 1½ to 2 in. long, flat on top with two white bands and a prominent midrib on underside, and sharp-pointed. Leaves on lower branches appear two-ranked because of twist at base of leaf. Cones 2⅜ to 4 in. long. Bracts extend beyond cone scales and end in elongated, needle-like spines ½ to 2 in. long, giving the cone a bristly appearance.

*Range:* Dry slopes of the Santa Lucia Mountains in Monterey County at elevations of 2,200 to 4,500 feet. May. Yellow Pine Forest, Broadleaf Evergreen Forest.

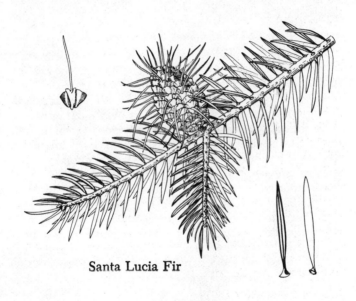

Santa Lucia Fir

# Redwood Family (Taxodiaceae)

Two species of redwoods are found in California today. Fossil evidence indicates that these species as well as several others now extinct were once widespread in North America, Europe, and Asia. Once considered to be the oldest living things on earth, redwoods are now placed second, behind the Bristlecone Pine. Redwoods are still considered the earth's largest living things, however. The Coast Redwood enters the area covered by this book only in Monterey County. The Big Tree or Giant Sequoia is confined to the central Sierra Nevada. Both species may be found as garden or street trees in many southern California cities.

## Coast Redwood (Sequoia sempervirens)

This is a spectacular forest tree, with some specimens in northern California reaching a height of over 350 ft. The columnar trunks of many mature trees are free of branches for 50 to 100 ft. and are usually strongly buttressed at the base. The pyramidal crowns of young trees tend to become rounded or sometimes open and nearly flat in old trees. Bark of mature trees is thick, soft, fibrous, and dark cinnamon-brown with a greyish tinge. They reproduce by seeds or crown root sprouts, grow rapidly and produce sizable trees in 60 to 70 years, and hence, if properly managed and controlled, should provide a perpetual supply of this valuable resource. The Coast Redwood has no tap root but does have a number of large lateral roots with a mass of feeder rootlets which lie near the surface. The accumulation of leaves and twigs which fall from the tree tend, over the years, to build a porous mat around and near the base of the tree. This serves to retain the moisture, supplied by rain and fog, which is so important to the life of these fast-growing trees. It also provides a suitable habitat for crown sprouts to develop. In order to preserve this essential provision of nature, no camping or picnicking should be allowed near the bases of these trees. The fenced-off no-man's land which has been created around the bases of many magnificent trees in our public parks is designed to preserve as nearly as possible a natural habitat so that these trees may survive the ever-increasing onslaught of careless visitors.

*Leaves and fruit:* Leaves of two kinds. On lower branches, leaves linear ½ to ¾ in. long, dark green above with two whitish bands beneath, short-petioled, two-ranked and forming flat sprays. On some upper shoots, leaves short, linear to awl-shaped, forming close spirals around the twig and resembling somewhat the leaves of *Sequoia gigantea.* Cones ½ to 1 in. long, thick woody scales, ripen the first year.

*Range:* Coastal fog belt from Santa Lucia Mountains to southwestern Oregon. March. Redwood Forest.

## CYPRESS FAMIILY (CUPRESSACEAE)

The members (genera) of the Cypress family found in this area are Incense Cedar *(Callocedrus),* cypresses *(Cupressus),* and junipers *(Juniperus).* They embrace many valuable and picturesque species which are found widespread throughout the state. Many species are extensively cultivated in parks and gardens. They all have closely adhering scale-like leaves.

### Incense Cedar *(Callocedrus decurrens)*

The Incense Cedar is a handsome, aromatic evergreen 75 to 150 ft. tall with a tapering trunk covered with thick fibrous cinnamon-brown bark, which somewhat resembles the trunk and bark of the giant Sequoia. Young trees are pyramidal. The crowns of the older trees are open and irregular. Leaf-bearing twigs tend to branch in one plane forming flat sprays which give the tree a lacy appearance. The wood is light, soft, and durable. It is used extensively in making shingles, posts, lead pencils, railroad ties, and many other useful products.

*Leaves and fruit:* Leaves simple, scale-shaped, ⅛ to 3/16 in. long, closely appressed to the branchlets, only the tips free. Cyclic, four-ranked, two outer rows keel-shaped and overlapping the two inner rows, highly aromatic when crushed. Cones ¾ to 1 in. long consisting of one pair of large seed-bearing scales separated from a closed center of 2 or 4 sharp-pointed scales, pendulous, maturing the first season.

*Range:* Yellow Pine forest from Baja California to Southern Oregon at elevations of 1,500 to 8,000 ft. April—May. Yellow Pine Forest.

CYPRESS (CUPRESSUS)

There are ten cypresses native to California, five of which are found in this area, all of which produce woody, generally globular cones which mature the second season and may remain on the tree for several seasons.

**Monterey Cypress** *(Cupressus macrocarpa)*

This is one of our most picturesque trees when silhouetted against the blue ocean or the white sand dunes in its restricted native habitat on the Monterey Peninsula, from which it derives its name. Its height, 40 to 70 ft., varies greatly depending on exposure. Young trees are sharply conical; as the tree matures it tends to spread out into a wide flat-topped or umbrella-shaped crown. Wood is fine-grained, heavy, and has a faint aromatic odor. The irregular shape of the tree and its limited quantity prevent the wood from becoming commercially important. It is extensively cultivated for windbreaks, hedges, and ornamentals, especially along the coast, due to its ability to survive on rather poor sandy soil and to withstand the ravages of the strong and cool coastal winds.

*Leaves and fruit:* Dark yellow-green, non-glandular, scale-like leaves 1/16 to 1/12 in. long, opposite each other in four rows and forming rope-like branchlets. Cones subglobose ¾ to 1¾ in. long, mature second season, remain on the tree for many years.

*Range:* Monterey Peninsula, principally in a narrow strip a few hundred feet wide from Point Pinos to Carmel and on Point Lobos. Closed-cone Pine Forest.

### Gowan Cypress *(Cupressus goveniana)*

This cypress is a small tree or tree-like shrub 3 to 20 ft. tall, which is rather sparsely branched. The bark on young trees and on the branches of old trees tends to be smooth and brown to grayish, while the bark on the trunks of old trees is rough and fibrous. This interesting cypress often develops a tiny pigmy form which will survive on very poor or nearly sterile soil and which may produce cones when it is only two or three feet tall.

*Leaves and fruit:* Rich green scale-like leaves about 1/16 to 1/12 in. long, bluntish and usually without visible dorsal resin pits. Cones subglobose about ½ in. long, remain closed for many years.

*Range:* Huckleberry Hill and San Jose Creek in Monterey County. Closed-cone Pine Forest.

### Cuyamaca Cypress *(Cupressus stephensonii)*

This is a small erect or spreading tree 25 to 50 ft. tall. Branchlets are thick, stiff, and tend to be squarish. The bark on mature trees is reddish and smooth and falls off in scales or strips. This is another of those interesting trees which are to be found only in highly restricted areas, sometimes referred to as tree islands.

*Leaves and fruit:* Blue-gray to gray-green scale-like leaves about 1/20 in. long, sharp-pointed, and with active dorsal resin pits. Cones ¾ to 1 in. long.

*Range:* Headwaters of King Creek on the southwest slope of Cuyamaca Peak in San Diego County. Chaparral.

[ 49 ]

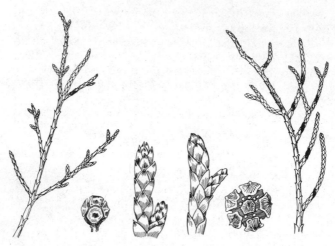

Sargent Cypress          Monterey Cypress

### Tecate Cypress *(Cupressus forbesii)*

A small tree 15 to 30 ft. tall, with an irregular spreading crown. The dark reddish-brown or cherry-red bark tends to fall off in thin scales or strips. This is another tree whose habitat is highly restricted.

*Leaves and fruit:* Rich- to dull-green scale-like leaves about 1/20 in. long, sharp-pointed, and obscurely glandular. Cones globose ¾ to 1¼ in. long, remaining closed for many years.

*Range:* Claymine and Gypsum canyons, Santa Ana Mountains in Orange County, and on Tecate, Otay, and Quatay Mountains in San Diego County. Chaparral.

### Sargent Cypress *(Cupressus sargentii)*

A small tree 10 to 40 ft. tall that is sometimes shrub-like and whose main trunk is usually straight. Its erect or spreading branches tend to form open crowns. Bark is grayish-dark-brown to almost black, thick, and fibrous. It is somewhat more widespread than several other species of cypresses.

*Leaves and fruit:* Dull-green scale-like leaves about 1/12 in. long, blunt. Some older leaves may have closed resin pits. Cones subglobose ¾ to 1 in. long.

*Range:* Zaca Peak in Santa Barbara County to Red Mountain in Mendocino County at elevations of 700 to 3,000 ft. Chaparral, Closed-cone Pine Forest.

JUNIPER (JUNIPERUS)

Junipers are closely related to the cypresses. It is often difficult to distinguish between them without the study of their fruits. The fruit of the juniper is an ovoid berry-like cone, usually covered with coalesced scales as contrasted with the fruit of the cypress which is a globular or subglobular woody cone. Both mature the second season.

## Western Juniper *(Juniperus occidentalis)*

Also known as Sierra Juniper. This is a very picturesque tree 20 to 60 ft. tall, often with a gnarled and grotesque form. It is one of the real monarchs of the high mountains and is readily recognized by its short, stocky, weatherbeaten, shreddy cinnamon-brown trunk and open crown. Young trees in protected areas have a straight, sharply-tapering open crown.

*Leaves and fruit:* Gray-green scale-like leaves about ⅛ in. long attached singly in circles of three, closely appressed, completely covering the twig and forming a rounded stem with six longitudinal rows of leaves. Each leaf marked on the back with a glandular resin pit, cones berry-like ¼ to 1/3 in. long, globular to oblong-ovoid, bluish-black with white bloom at maturity.

*Range:* San Bernardino Mountains at elevations of 6,700 to 10,000 ft., north through the Sierra Nevada to Modoc and Siskiyou counties at elevations of 3,000 to

10,000 ft. Yellow Pine Forest, Lodgepole Pine—White Fir Forest.

### California Juniper *(Juniperus californica)*

A small tree 20 to 30 ft. tall, usually with several secondary trunks emerging from near the base and with a broad open crown. Bark is ashy-gray in contrast to the cinnamon-brown bark of the Western Juniper, with which it is sometimes confused.

*Leaves and fruit:* Scale-like leaves similar to those of the Western Juniper execpt more bluntish. Cones berry-like, globose to oblong, ⅜ to ⅝ in. long, reddish-brown under whitish bloom when mature.

*Range:* Frequently associated with One Leaf Piñon Pine on the western slope of the Colorado Desert (Joshua Tree National Monument), western slope of southern Sierra Nevada and Santa Lucia Mountains. January—March. Piñon—Juniper Woodland, Joshua Tree—High Desert Woodland.

### Utah Juniper *(Juniperus osteosperma)*

This is a small tree or tree-like shrub 10—15 ft. tall, usually with a short or several-stemmed trunk, sometimes called Desert Juniper. It is very similar to California Juniper except that it ordinarily has a rounded crown, giving the appearance of small round green clumps on the hillsides.

*Leaves and fruit:* Scale-shaped leaves 1/10 to ⅛ in. long, tending to be sharp-pointed, attached singly in circles of 2 or 3 around the twig, usually without glands. Cones berry-like, globular 3/16 to ⅜ in. long, reddish-brown under whitish bloom when mature.

*Range:* Associated with One Leaf Piñon Pine on dry slopes and flats at 4,800 to 8,500 feet from east Mojave Desert to Bridgeport area. Piñon—Juniper Woodland, Joshua Tree—High Desert Woodland.

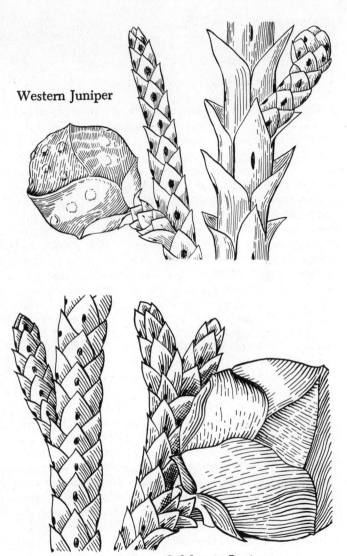

Western Juniper

California Juniper

# BROADLEAF TREES

Southern California has a variety of native broadleaf trees. The most common are the alders, maples, oaks, poplars, sycamore, and willows. There also are many rare and unusual species such as the dogwoods, elderberries, mesquites, palms, palo verde, smoke tree, and yuccas, to mention just a few. At certain times of the year the buckeye, dogwoods, elderberries, flannel bush, oaks, poplars, redbud, smoke tree, and yuccas add much to the color of our California landscape by the varied and brilliant hues of their flowers, fruits, and foliage. Most native broadleaf trees in southern California, except certain oaks and maples, have comparatively little commercial value except for firewood and novelties. However, many have real esthetic value and are cultivated extensively as street or park trees. Undoubtedly their greatest value lies in the beauty and charm which they lend to the California landscape. What is more picturesque than our rolling foothills dotted with spreading Coast Live Oak, or our moist high mountain slopes covered in the fall of the year with a blanket of bright yellow Quaking Aspen silhouetted against a background of green pine or fir, or the brilliant red coloration of the Mountain Dogwood after the first onset of cold weather? Every legitimate effort should be made to preserve as much as possible of California's natural beauty consistent with a well-developed over-all utilization pattern, recognizing that nature once destroyed can never be reestablished within one's lifetime.

Leaf descriptions as used in this section refer to the characteristics of the leaf blade only unless otherwise indicated.

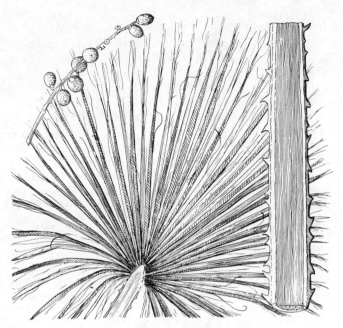

California Fan Palm

## Palm Family (Palmaceae)

**California Fan Palm** *(Washingtonia filifera)*

Also known as Desert Palm. This is a characteristically column-like and unbranched tree 30 to 60 ft. tall. The upper part of the trunk, which is just below a bushy crown composed of a cluster of spreading fan-like leaves, is usually covered with a dense thatch of large dead leaves. The lower part of the trunk tends to become smooth with horizontal ridges. It is the only palm which is indigenous to California and is widely cultivated as an ornamental in the arid areas of the state due to its ability to survive extreme heat and long dry periods. Palms and yuccas differ structurally from other California trees in that their woody tissues are not arranged in annual concentric rings but are scattered irregularly in thread-like fibers throughout the trunk. Their picturesque and somewhat top-heavy silhouette forms an interesting and characteristic sight when viewed against the somber background of the desert and the distant dark hills and mountains of their natural habitat.

*Leaves, flowers, and fruit:* Leaves gray-green, 3 to 6 ft. long, with deeply slashed folds terminating in sharp thread-like filaments, petioles 3 to 6 ft. long, armed along the margins with short hook-like spines; small whitish flowers borne in large clusters 8 to 10 ft. long; fruit abundant, berry-like, hard, ovoid ⅜ to ½ in. long, blackish when ripe; seeds chestnut-brown.

*Range:* Scattered groves in canyons and seeps of the Colorado and southern Mojave deserts, Palm Canyon near Palm Springs, Joshua Tree National Monument near Park Headquarters. June. Creosote Bush—Low Desert Scrub, Riparian Woodland.

AGAVE FAMILY (AGAVACEAE)

**Joshua Tree** *(Yucca brevifolia)*

An unusual-looking tree 15 to 30 ft. tall. Mature trees have a columnar trunk with many thick and bristly branches. Young trees are without branches until they produce their first flowers, then frequently two branches develop, each of which will generally produce two more branches, this continuing until a much-branched and open crown is formed. The bark, where free of leaves, is reddish-brown to gray and checked into small squarish plates. It is easily the most weird-looking denizen of the California deserts. The approach to a Joshua Tree forest on a bright moonlit night presents a never-to-be-forgotten sight. The sharp-pointed bayonet-like leaves, which adhere to the stem and branches for many years, defy intrusion from

[ 56 ]

would-be animal enemies who, in this otherwise barren area, would feed on its foliage. This protective provision is one factor which has made possible the survival of this fascinating inhabitant of arid country. It is fortunate that the federal government has set aside the Joshua Tree National Monument to preserve in its natural habitat this interesting and most unusual tree.

*Leaves, flowers, and fruit:* Leaves, bluish-green, stiff, 6 to 10 in. long, 2 in. or less wide at the base, tapering to a very sharp point, edges with minute teeth throughout, persisting for many years. Stems and branches, except old trunks, covered with close thatch of dead leaves; flowers, greenish-white, fleshy, waxen, rather ill-smelling, about 2 in. long, borne at the end of the crown branches in a single stiff and branched cluster about 1 ft. long; fruit is a capsule, 2 to 4 in. long, plump, with 6 chambers filled with flat black seeds, becoming dry and dropping when mature, scattered by wind.

*Range:* Mojave Desert to Owens Valley, 2,000 to 6,000 ft. elevation. April—May. Joshua Tree—High Desert Woodland.

## Mojave Yucca *(Yucca schidigera)*

Also known as Spanish Dagger. A small strange tree, 5 to 15 ft. tall, with a single or occasionally branched trunk. The bark, where free of dead leaves, is dark brown, cross-checked, and furrowed. This is another of the interesting and unusual trees which are indigenous to the hot arid areas of southern California.

*Leaves, flowers, and fruit:* Leaves yellow-green, 1½ to 3 ft. long, 2 to 3 in. wide at base, tapering to sharp point, margins entire with few curled shreddy filaments, stiff; flowers, white to cream, borne in a single-branched cluster, 1 to 1½ ft. long; fruit is a capsule, 2 to 4 in. long, with 6 chambers filled with black seeds.

[ 57 ]

*Range:* Dry slopes, mesas, and desert areas of San Diego, Riverside, and San Bernardino counties, usually below 5,000 ft. April—May. Sagebrush Scrub, Creosote Bush—Low Desert Scrub, Chaparral.

Wax Myrtle

## Wax Myrtle Family (Myricaceae)

**Wax Myrtle** *(Myrica californica)*

A small evergreen tree 10 to 30 ft. tall with slender ascending branches and smooth gray to light brown bark. It is frequently many-stemmed and quite shrub-like.

*Leaves and fruit:* Leaves simple, alternate, 2 to 5 in. long, oblong to oblanceolate, dark green above, undersurface slightly lighter and minutely dotted with almost microscopic resin glands, remotely serrated to almost entire, narrowed at base to short petiole; fruit a small, hard, purplish-brown berry-like nut about ¼ in. in diameter, coated with a whitish wax, borne in short auxiliary clusters.

*Range:* Canyons, moist slopes, and flats below 500 feet from the Santa Monica Mountains north to Washington. March–April. Coastal Scrub, Redwood Forest, Riparian Woodland.

## Walnut Family (Juglandaceae)

**California Walnut** *(Juglans californica)*

This is a small tree 15 to 30 ft. tall which frequently has several trunks branching from near the ground, giving the tree a somewhat bushy or shrub-like appearance. Trunks of mature trees are dark brown with broad irregular ridges.

*Leaves and fruit:* Leaves pinnately compound, 6 to 10 in. long with 11 to 15 sessile finely serrated smooth leaflets 1 to 2 in. long and 1/3 to ¾ in. wide; fruit, a spherical, thick-shelled, shallow-grooved nut ½ to ¾ in. in diameter and surrounded with a dark brown pubescent husk, somewhat similar in appearance to the nut of the cultivated English Walnut, although much smaller and thicker-shelled.

*Range:* Santa Ana Mountains eastward to the foothills of the San Bernardino Mountains and north to Santa Barbara County. April–May. Southern Oak Woodland.

California Walnut

## WILLOW FAMILY (SALICACEAE)

The willow family includes two genera, the poplars and the willows. Members of this family produce spike-like masses of flowers known as catkins. These catkins are of two types, male and female. Plants of a genus, such as the willows, which produce only male (staminate) flowers on one individual tree and only female (pistillate) flowers on another tree of the same species, are called dioecious plants. Other plants, such as oaks, produce separate male and female flowers on the same tree and are called monoecious plants. The seeds are attached to extremely fine silk-like or cottony hairs which permit the wind to carry them a considerable distance and thus provide for a wide distribution of these trees. The leaves of all members of this family are simple and are borne alternately on the twig. Since the leaves drop in the fall the trees are known as deciduous rather than evergreen. Poplars and willows are commonly found along stream beds, or in relatively moist places. To the early pioneer they were a welcome sight, since in most cases their presence indicated that water was near at hand and that a shallow well would produce at least a limited supply of that most essential resource. They grow readily from root sprouts, seeds, or cuttings. In certain parts of the country it is not an uncommon sight to see a row of willows or poplars which are the remnants of an old fence line, having sprouted from green posts driven in the ground. Also, in the early days, willows and poplars were extensively planted as windbreaks, due primarily to the fact that they are extremely hardy and grew very rapidly. They also provided shade, fence posts, firewood, and some low-grade lumber.

### POPLAR (POPULUS)

This genus includes Aspen and the cottonwoods.

**Aspen** *(Populus tremuloides)*

Also known as Quaking Aspen. This is a slender tree 10 to 60 ft. tall with a smooth greenish-white bark. Its leaf stalks are slender and flattened, allowing the leaves to flutter in the breeze, which accounts for its common name. The Aspen is responsible for much of the brilliant yellow coloration which we see in our high, wet mountain meadows and slopes in the autumn and early winter. Aspen, with their white trunks and shimmering green leaves, are equally spectacular in summer. In winter the white trunks stand out in contrast to their usual green or gray background.

*Leaves:* Dull green on upper surface, paler on under surface, 1 to 2½ in. long and nearly as wide, broadly ovate with a short sharp point at the apex, margins finely or only slightly toothed.

*Range:* Widely distributed along stream banks, meadows, and damp slopes throughout the higher and cooler regions of North America. In southern California along Fish Creek in the San Bernardino Mountains. April—June. Riparian Woodlands, bordering Mountain Meadows.

Aspen                    Fremont Cottonwood

### Fremont Cottonwood *(Populus fremontii)*

This cottonwood is a handsome tree 40 to 90 ft. tall with a broad open crown. It is usually found along stream banks or beds and in moist places below 6,500 ft. Although the leaf stalk is flattened, it is somewhat thicker and heavier than the leaf stalk of the Aspen, and fluttering of the leaf blades is not as characteristic as with the Aspen. Its wood is fine-grained, soft, brittle, and has little commercial value except for fuel.

*Leaves:* Yellowish-green on upper surface, lighter on under surface, 1½ to 3½ in. long and as wide, broadly ovate, tending to be broadly heart-shaped or flattish

[ 62 ]

at the base, tapering to a point at apex. Leaf stems 1½ to 3 in. long, flattened, and yellowish.

*Range:* Moist mountain and desert slopes of southern California, and in coastal areas of central California. March—April. Riparian Woodland, Cismontane Rural, Southern Desert Wash, Desert Canal, Colorado River Bottom, Desert Rural bordering Freshwater Marsh.

### Black Cottonwood *(Populus trichocarpa)*

This is a big cottonwood, 40 to 150 ft. tall, with spreading branches forming a broad, open crown. Its grayish bark becomes darker and furrowed with age. The trunks of mature trees are usually free of branches for a considerable distance above the ground. This, like the other poplars, prefers a moist habitat, hence it is frequently found along the banks of living streams or freshwater lakes. The wood is soft, straight-grained and has some limited commercial use. The poplar was most widely planted by the early settlers as a shade or windbreak tree in newly developed areas. Leaves vary considerably in size and shape depending on soil conditions, temperature, and moisture.

*Leaves:* 2½ to 5 in. long, 2 to 3 in. wide, shiny dark green above, much paler beneath, margins finely toothed, broadest near base, and pointed towards apex. Occasionally leaves may be less than 2 in. wide and somewhat lance-shaped. Leaf stalks 1¼ to 2 in. long, stout and rounded.

*Range:* Widely distributed along the Pacific Coast from southern Alaska to southern California and from sea level to nearly 8,000 ft. elevation. February—April. Riparian Woodland.

There are numerous species and many varieties of willows in southern California, but only those that have definite tree-like characteristics will be treated in this volume. Anyone interested in an exhaustive study of these interesting trees should consult a comprehensive treatment of the genus. Many species and varieties which are shrubby under certain conditions may be tree-like in a more favorable environment.

### Red Willow (Salix laevigata)

A medium-sized tree 15 to 40 ft. tall, native along streams where it is frequently associated with the Golden Willow. It may be shrubby when growing under adverse conditions. The foliage at a. distance appears grizzled when the wind turns up the whitish under surface of the leaves. Bark of mature trees is usually dark and rough, while bark on young branches may be reddish-brown.

*Leaves and flowers:* Leaves variable, 2½ to 6 in. long, ¾ to 1⅛ in. wide, usually about 4 to 5 times as long as wide, rich green and shining above. Glaucous on under surface at maturity, margins only slightly toothed, lanceolate, and usually widest below the middle, although new leaves may be widest above the middle or near the tip, not long-tapering, rather thick and firm. Leaf stalk without glands; catkins slender—1¼ to 4 in. long.

*Range:* Coast Range in southern California from sea level to 4,000 feet. March—May. Riparian Woodland, bordering Freshwater Marsh.

### Golden Willow (Salix lasiandra)

This is a graceful tree 15 to 40 ft. tall although it may sometimes appear shrubby. It is native along streams where it is frequently associated with the Red Willow. The bark of a mature tree is dark and rough with interlacing ridges. One-year-old branches tend to be yellowish.

*Lodgepole Pine*     *Bishop Pine*

*Western Yellow Pine*     *Jeffrey Pine*

PLATE 1

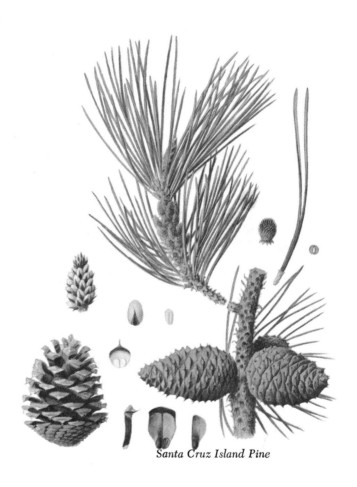

*Santa Cruz Island Pine*

PLATE 2

*Digger Pine*

*Coulter Pine*

*Monterey Pine*

*Knobcone Pine*

PLATE 3

*Sugar Pine*

*Bristlecone Pine*

*Douglas Fir*

*Big Cone Spruce*

PLATE 4

*White Fir*

*Coast Redwood*

*Incense Cedar*

*Gowen Cypress*

PLATE 5

*Cuyamaca Cypress*

*Tecate Cypress*

*Utah Juniper*

*Black Cottonwood*

PLATE 6

*Joshua Tree*

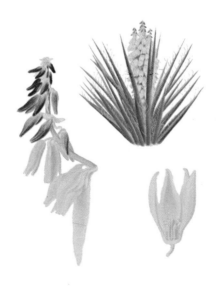

*Mojave Yucca*

PLATE 7

*Red Willow*

*Golden Willow*

*Black Willow*

*Arroyo Willow*

PLATE 8

*Nuttall Willow*          *Sandbar Willow*

*Red Alder*          *Tanbark Oak*

PLATE 9

*Valley Oak*

PLATE 10

*Blue Oak*

*Engelmann Oak*

*Canyon Live Oak*

*Coast Live Oak*

PLATE 11

*Interior Live Oak*　　　　　　*California Black Oak*

*Oracle Oak*　　　　　　*Palmer Oak*

PLATE 12

*California Laurel*

*Hard Tack*

*Desert Apricot*

*Hollyleaf Cherry*

PLATE 13

*Toyon*

*Western Redbud*

*Little Leaf Horse-Bean*

*Mexican Flannel Bush*

PLATE 14

*Smoke Tree*

PLATE 15

*Mountain Dogwood*          *Bigberry Manzanita*

*Arizona Ash*          *Blue Elderberry*

PLATE 16

*Leaves and flowers:* Leaves 3 to 6 in. long, ¾ to 1¼ in. wide, lanceolate, widest below middle and often long-tapering, dark green above, glaucous on undersurface at maturity, margins finely toothed. Leaf stalks ¾ to 1¼ in. long with tiny bead-like glands near base of leaf, half-moon-shaped stipules at base of leaf stalk. Catkins stout, about 1¼ to 3 in. long.

*Range:* Widespread throughout California on stream banks and moist places, below 8,000 ft. Not found as a native on deserts. March—May. Riparian Woodland.

### Black Willow *(Salix gooddingii)*

A medium-sized willow 20 to 40 ft. tall, sometimes shrubby. It is usually found along stream banks and wet places below 2,000 ft. Trunks of mature trees tend to be dark and rough. Twigs tend to be yellowish.

*Leaves and flowers:* Leaves linear-lanceolate, 2¼ to 4 in. long and ¼ in. or less wide, long, tapering, and rather thin. Margins closely and finely toothed, tending to be grayish-green on both surfaces. Young leaves usually pubescent. Leaf stalks ⅛ to ⅜ in. long, without glands. Catkins slender, 1 to 2½ in. long.

*Range:* Stream banks and wet places in southern California below 2,000 ft. Colorado River drainage area. March—April. Riparian Woodland, Colorado River Bottom.

### Arroyo Willow *(Salix lasiolepis)*

This is a small tree 10 to 30 ft. tall, sometimes quite shrubby. Usually it is found on borders of living or summer-dry streams, or in arroyos. Bark of mature trees is dark gray. Twigs are yellowish to reddish-brown and not widely diverging.

*Leaves and flowers:* Leaves oblanceolate 2½ to 5 in. long, ⅜ to 1¼ in. wide, dark green, and smooth above, hairy to smooth beneath, margins sometimes toothed and slightly rolled under. Catkins sessile, 1¼ to 2½ in. long.

*Range:* Coast Range up to 4,000 ft. in southern California. February—April. Riparian Woodland.

**Nuttall Willow** *(Salix scouleriana)*

This is a small tree 10 to 30 ft. tall, sometimes shrubby. The bark on the trunks of mature trees is dull gray to blackish. Its twigs are stoutish and vary from yellowish to brownish-black. It is found along stream banks and in moist places up to an elevation of 10,000 ft.

*Leaves and flowers:* Leaves 1½ to 3½ in. long, ½ to 1½ in. wide, variable in shape, usually widest above middle, either very short-pointed or rounded at apex, thin, yellow-green and smooth above, silvery pubescent to smooth on paler under surface, margins entire or sometimes slightly toothed, leaf stalks ¼ to ½ in. long. Catkins 1 to 2 in. long and very showy.

*Range:* Along streams and in moist places from southern California to Alaska below 10,000 ft. April—June. Riparian Woodland.

**Watson's Willow** *(Salix lutea var. watsonii)*

A small tree 8 to 15 ft. tall, frequently occurring as a clustered shrub. Twigs are widely diverging, brittle, pipe-clay in color, and very smooth.

*Leaves and flowers:* Leaves 1½ to 2½ in. long, ½ to 1¼ in. wide, widest near middle or towards base, margins entire to serrate, rich green on upper surface, paler and glaucous beneath, stipules ovate to crescent-shaped. Catkins 1 to 1½ in. long, appearing before or with leaves in May—June.

*Range:* San Jacinto and San Bernardino Mountains. May—June. Riparian Woodland.

**Sandbar Willow** *(Salix hindsiana)*

Sometimes known as Valley Willow or Gray Narrow Leaf Willow. A small tree 10 to 20 ft. tall, frequently quite shrubby. The bark on mature trees is gray and furrowed. Bark on young twigs is gray and hairy. It is common along ditches, sandbars, river banks, and in flood beds.

*Leaves and flowers:* Leaves 1¾ to 3½ in. long, ⅛ to ¼ in. wide, linear, tapering at both ends, sometimes hairy on both surfaces, sometimes only on lower surface, sometimes not hairy at all but green and smooth, leaf stalks ⅛ in. or less long. Catkins 1 to 1½ in. long, tipped with short styles and long stigmas.

*Range:* San Diego County to Oregon below 3,000 ft. March—May. Riparian Woodland.

## Birch Family (Betulaceae)

Alders are the only members of the Birch family in southern California which normally attain tree size. There are two species of these interesting "cone-bearing" broadleaf trees which are native to this area. The leaves of these water-loving trees, which usually are found on or near the banks of live streams, are simple, alternate, and deciduous. They have conspicuous straight and parallel side veins which extend from the midrib to the margin of the leaf. The male flowers appear as catkins and hang pendulously from the ends of the branchlets. The female flowers, or "cones," of the alders are usually found in clusters and drop as entire cones while those of the Water Birch, with which the alder may sometimes be confused, are solitary and distintegrate on the tree. Alder cones, either sprayed or natural, make interesting and attractive holiday decorations.

### White Alder *(Alnus rhombifolia)*

This is a graceful tree 30 to 100 ft. tall, and usually with a straight trunk and spreading branches. Its whitish or grayish-brown bark is characteristically broken into irregular plates on old trees. White Alders are frequently planted as park trees and, when sufficient space and moisture are available, develop into handsome specimens. The wood has limited use except as firewood.

*Leaves and fruit:* Leaves ovate 2 to 4 in. long, 1½ to 2 in. wide, often larger on new sprouts, dark green above, yellow-green and minutely hairy beneath; leaf margins finely to irregularly toothed to coarsely to doubly toothed; margins not rolled under, which helps to distinguish it from the Red Alder. Mature cones usually less than ¾ in. long.

*Range:* The common alder along inland and mountain streams, mostly below 5,000 ft., not common along the coast, although it may be found with the Red Alder along the banks of some coastal streams. January—April. Riparian Woodland.

### Red Alder  *(Alnus oregona)*

Also known as Oregon Alder. This is a medium-sized tree 40 to 80 ft. tall with slender, spreading, and somewhat pendulous branches. It has a whitish or pale-gray outer bark and a reddish-brown inner bark. Its fine-grained wood, which somewhat resembles maple, has some commercial use for box wood, furniture making, novelties, and the like. At first glance it is frequently confused with the more widely-distributed White Alder. However, on careful observation a number of differences become apparent. Leaves and cones of the Red Alder are usually somewhat the larger. Leaf margins of the Red Alder are slightly rolled under, giving the impression of a very narrow green rim around the margin on the under surface. The leaf margins of the White Alder have no such rolled-under edge. Leaves of the White Alder are ovate while those of the Red Alder tend to be elliptic-ovate. Bark of the Red Alder tends to be smoother and more mottled.

*Leaves and fruit:* Leaves 2½ to 6 in. long, 1½ to 3 in. wide, ovate to elliptic-ovate, dark green, smooth

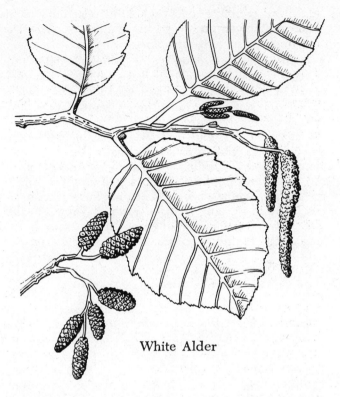

White Alder

or slightly hairy on upper surface, usually rusty-hairy on under surface, margins coarsely toothed, large teeth further finely toothed; cones usually more than ¾ in. long.

*Range:* Stream banks and moist flats near the coast from Alaska to San Luis Obispo County. March–April. Riparian Woodland.

## Beech Family (Fagaceae)

The Beech Family includes three members (genera), Chinquapin *(Castanopsis)*, Tanbark Oak *(Lithocarpus)*, and Oak *(Quercus)*.

## Golden Chinquapin
*(Castanopsis chrysophylla var. minor)*

A small evergreen tree or shrub 15 to 25 ft. tall, with ascending or spreading branches forming a rounded crown. The Golden Chinquapin resembles somewhat the chestnuts of the eastern United States both in leaf form and fruit structure.

*Leaves, flowers, and fruit:* Leaves simple, alternate, 2 to 3 in. long, ½ to 1¼ in. wide, usually folded upward along the midrib producing a trough-like effect, entire, oblong to oblong-lanceolate, thick, leathery, dark green above, golden-brown beneath. Flowers monoecious, both male and female catkins borne on the same tree, creamy-white in erect catkins 1½ to 2½ in. long. Fruit chestnut-like burs almost enclosing a shiny light-brown nut containing a reddish, sweet kernel.

*Range:* Coast Ranges from Santa Lucia Mountains north to Del Norte and Siskiyou Mountains. June–September. Broadleaf Evergreen Forest, Chaparral.

### Tanbark Oak *(Lithocarpus densiflora)*

This is a broadleaf evergreen tree 50 to 120 ft. tall with a thick gray-green and usually furrowed bark. Tanbark has long been an important source of tannin for use in the leather industry, although, in recent years many other sources of tannin have been developed to supply the increased demand for this important material. Young branches are densely covered with short, soft hairs. This is not a true oak, but a near relative.

*Leaves and fruit:* Simple alternate leaves 2 to 5 in. long, ¾ to 2½ in. wide, oblong with blunt apex, prominent parallel side veins ending in sharp points, reddish-yellow new leaves covered with a whitish or rusty fuzz which tends to disappear, leaving the upper surface smooth or nearly so. Ill-smelling catkins 2½ to 4 in. long; fruit an ovoid acorn ¾ to 1 in. long with a

[ 70 ]

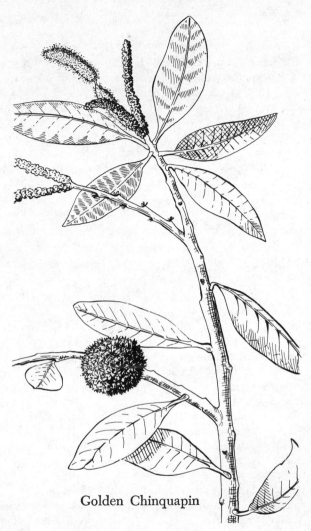

Golden Chinquapin

shallow, bristly cup, like those of the true Oaks (see below), maturing the second season.

*Range:* Wooded slopes of Coast Range from Ventura County to southern Oregon and also on western slope of Sierra Nevada below 4,500 ft. June–October. Broad-leaf Evergreen Forest, Redwood Forest.

The oaks represent one of the most picturesque and widespread groups of broadleaf trees in California. Some are small trailing shrubs while others are large spreading trees, some are deciduous and others are evergreen, some grow at sea level, some in the high mountains. The fruit of the oak is an acorn composed of two parts—a rounded, smooth-shelled nut, pointed at the outer end, and a scaly saucer or cup enclosing the base of the nut. The acorns of certain species furnished an important item of food for the early Indians. Eight of the eleven California species classed as trees are found in southern California.

### Valley Oak (Quercus lobata)

A large, graceful, deciduous tree 50 to 120 ft. tall with wide-spreading and somewhat pendulous outer branches. Its thick dark-gray bark is checkered and usually covered with light gray scales. Many fine specimens are being indiscriminately cut for firewood, a practice which should be discouraged in order to preserve this picturesque aspect of our landscape.

*Leaves and fruit:* Leaves 2½ to 5 in. long, 2 to 4 in. wide, mainly oblong with 9 to 11 deep rounded lobes, not spiny, upper surface dull green and finely pubescent, tending to become smooth as leaves mature, under surface paler, pubescent, and yellow-veined. Acorns 1¼ to 2 in. long, ½ to ¾ in. thick, cup deeply hemispherical with warty scales near base, maturing the first year.

*Range:* Sacramento, San Joaquin, and adjacent valleys, inner and middle coastal ranges to San Fernando Valley. March—April. Oak Woodland, Southern Oak Woodland.

### Blue Oak (Quercus douglasii)

A medium-sized deciduous tree 20 to 60 ft. tall with grayish, checked bark. Its short, stout branches tend to form a rounded crown. It is frequently associated with the Digger Pine.

*Leaves and fruit:* Leaves oblong to obovate, 1½ to 4 in. long, ¾ to 2 in. wide, shallowly and irregularly lobed or not lobed at all, smooth to minutely pubescent, bluish-green above, paler underneath. Acorns commonly ovoid ¾ to 1¼ in. long, shallow cups with small warty scales, maturing the first year.

*Range:* Dry slopes bordering interior valleys from Los Angeles County to head of Sacramento Valley. April—May. Oak Woodland, Southern Oak Woodland.

### Engelmann Oak *(Quercus engelmannii)*

Also known as Mesa Oak. This is a small to medium-sized evergreen tree 15 to 50 ft. tall, the bark covered within grayish scales. Its spreading branches tend to form a rounded crown similar to that of the Blue Oak. It will occasionally hybridize with the Valley Oak and Scrub Oak.

*Leaves and fruit:* Leaves oblong to obovate, 1 to 3 in. long, ½ to 1 in. wide, leaf margins entire, wavy, or slightly toothed, grayish-blue-green, smooth or slightly pubescent above; paler, smooth or pubescent beneath. Acorns ovoid, blunt, ¾ to 1 in. long, cup shallow to bowl-shaped, mature the first season.

*Range:* Foothills below 4,000 ft. from Pasadena region to San Dimas and south to eastern San Diego County. Not found near the coast. April—May. Southern Oak Woodland.

### Canyon Live Oak *(Quercus chrysolepis)*

Also known as Maul Oak, Gold Cup Oak, or Iron Oak. This is another of our interesting and highly variable evergreen oaks. It may be found growing as a small shrub on a high, dry exposure or as a massive tree 60 to 70 ft. tall in a moist canyon or open flat. Its sturdy, spreading, and somewhat irregular branches tend to form a widespread or, occasionally, a rounded crown. The wood is heavy, hard, tough, and strong. It was used by the early settlers for making mauls, wagon tongues, wheel stock, and parts of certain farm implements. Its characteristic leaves usually persist for 3 to 4 years. The bark of the mature tree is dark gray and scaly. Young twigs are usually covered with woolly hairs or may be quite smooth.

*Leaves and fruit:* Leaves variable; usually oblong, 1 to 3 in. long, ½ to 1½ in. wide, margins entire or toothed, stiff, leathery, bluish-green above, underside of young leaves covered with a yellow powdery material, year-old leaves dull gray and smooth beneath. Leaves on young vigorous sprouts quite spiny; acorns oblong, ovoid, 1 to 1¼ in. long, cups more or less turban-shaped, first-season cups usually covered with a yellow powdery fuzz. Acorns mature the second season.

*Range:* Widely distributed in canyons, moist slopes and flats below 6,500 ft. from southern Oregon to Baja California. April—May. Riparian Woodland and many other plant communities.

## Coast Live Oak *(Quercus agrifolia)*

Also known as California Live Oak. A picturesque evergreen tree 30 to 75 ft. tall with great spreading stout branches, forming a broad-headed crown. It is another of those magnificent trees whose primary value lies in the charm which they lend to the California landscape. It has some limited use as a street or park tree.

*Leaves and fruit:* Leaves oblong to oval or broadly elliptical, 1 to 3 in. long, ¾ to 1¾ in. wide, stiff, leathery, frequently convex on upper surface, usually spiny, dark green and glossy on upper surface, under surface paler and usually with a tiny patch of brown or gray fuzz in angles formed by midrib and side veins. Acorns mature in first year. Cup turban-like, nut slender and pointed, 1 to 1½ in. long.

*Range:* Common in valleys and foothills of Coast Range from Sonoma County to San Diego County.

March—April. Southern Oak Woodland, Broadleaf Evergreen Forest.

### Interior Live Oak *(Quercus wislizenii)*

A beautiful evergreen tree 25 to 75 ft. tall with stout, spreading branches forming a rounded crown. In the San Jacinto Mountains and farther south, it may appear quite shrubby. It has been used to a limited extent as a park or street tree; when sufficient space and care are provided it will develop into a handsome specimen. It, like the Coast Live Oak, lends beauty and charm to our rolling foothills.

*Leaves and fruit:* Leaves 1 to 3 in. long, ¾ to 1¾ in. wide, stiff, leathery, oblong, illiptical, ovate to lanceolate, entire to spiny, usually flattish, upper surface dark green, under surface yellowish-green, smooth, no fuzz at junction of midrib and side veins. Acorns mature second season. Cup turban-like to cup-shaped. Nut 1 to 1½ in. long, slender, oblong and pointed.

*Range:* Rolling foothills of the central valleys and inner Coast Range, Santa Ana Range, San Bernardino, San Jacinto, and Cuyamaca Mountains, usually below 5,000 ft. March—May. Southern Oak Woodland, Chaparral.

### California Black Oak *(Quercus kelloggii)*

A deciduous oak 30 to 80 ft. tall, its spreading branches forming a broad, rounded crown. Leaves on young shoots at higher elevations tend to be reddish in early spring. Leaves in the fall turn yellow to almost bright-red producing a spectacular color effect when silhouetted against a varied and somewhat drab background.

*Leaves and fruit:* Leaves broadly elliptical to obovate, 4 to 7 in. long, 2 to 4 in. wide. Lobes deep and sharp-pointed, each point tipped with a soft bristle. Mature leaves smooth and dark green on upper surface, paler on under surface. Young leaves may be hairy or woolly on both surfaces. Acorns mature second year. Cups wider than deep, slightly hairy on inner

[ 75 ]

surface. Nuts 1 to 1⅛ in. long, cylindrical, rounded at apex.

*Range:* Sierra Nevada and Coast Ranges from San Diego County to Oregon, usually at elevations of 1,000 to 8,000 ft. April—May. Yellow Pine Forest.

## Oracle Oak *(Quercus morehus)*

A small evergreen tree 20 to 40 ft. tall, which is sometimes quite shrubby. It is usually found near the California Black Oak and Interior Live Oak and is considered a hybrid of these species. Its acorns are quite similar to those of the Interior Live Oak, while its leaves are somewhat similar to those of the California Black Oak. Leaves persist until new leaves appear.

*Leaves and fruit:* Leaves 2 to 4 in. long, 1 to 2 in. wide, oblong to elliptical, with sharp, shallow, forward-pointing lobes tipped with a spine, dark green and smooth above, paler beneath. Acorns mature second season. Cup turban-like to cup-shaped, nut slender, ¾ to 1¼ in. long.

*Range:* Scattered on slopes and foothills of Sierra Nevada and Coast Range from San Diego County to Trinity and Eldorado counties below 5,000 ft. Southern Oak Woodland, Yellow Pine Forest.

## Palmer Oak *(Quercus palmeri)*

A small evergreen tree or shrub 6 to 18 ft. tall. It is usually found at the edge of chaparral thickets.

*Leaves and fruit:* Leaves ½ to 1½ in. long, stiff, curled, gray-green above. May be slightly hairy beneath, especially when young. Acorn cup shallow, silky within, densely hairy on the outside. Nut 1 to 1½ in. long, acute.

*Range:* San Luis Obispo County, San Bernardino and San Jacinto Mountains usually at elevations of 3,000 to 5,000 ft. April—May. Chaparral.

## Laurel Family (Lauraceae)

**California Laurel** *(Umbellularia californica)*

Also known in various localities as California Bay, Bay Laurel, Pepperwood, or Oregon Myrtle. This is an evergreen tree which may reach a height of 90 ft. or more in the northern part of the range or may be shrubby when found growing in dry places. Its ascending and spreading branches tend to form a broad, rounded crown when it is found in a relatively open stand. When crowded its crown may be open and irregular. Its crushed leaves emit a pungently aromatic odor suggesting camphor or bay, which serves as a positive identifying characteristic. Leaves are often used for flavor in cooking. The wood is heavy, hard, firm, fine-grained, rich yellowish-brown, and frequently beautifully mottled. It is extensively used in the production of novelties and souvenirs such as plates, bowls, ash trays, figures, and the like. It is also used in the manufacture of some types of furniture. Since the wood is in such high demand and its supply is limited, serious consideration should be given to its most effective use, as well as to some satisfactory method of providing a continuous supply of this unique material.

*Leaves and fruit:* Leaves 3 to 5 in. long, ¾ to 1½ in. wide, oblong-lanceolate or lanceolate, smooth, thick, leathery, and entire; fruit a yellowish-green ovoid drupe, purplish when mature, about 1 in. long.

*Range:* Canyon slopes and along streams of Coast Range and Sierra Nevada from San Diego County to Oregon, below 5,000 ft. December—May. Riparian Woodland, Broadleaf Evergreen Forest, Southern Oak Woodland.

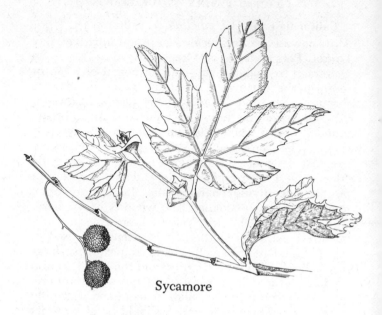

Sycamore

## Sycamore Family ( Platanaceae )

### Western Sycamore *(Platanus racemosa)*

Also known as Plane Tree. This is large conspicuous, deciduous tree 40 to 90 ft. tall, often with stout twisted branches forming an irregular open crown. In open areas one will frequently find an old tree with large, heavy, and crooked branches which have developed near the ground, producing a challenge to the venture-some tree-climbing boy as well as adding charm to the surroundings. Its dull brownish bark near the base is often quite furrowed and ridged, while a short distance above and on all branches it is smooth and ashy-white with greenish-gray patches. This is a good identifying characteristic. It is commonly found along stream beds and water courses in the drier areas of California, but not on the desert.

[ 78 ]

*Leaves and fruit:* Leaves 5 to 10 in. long, 6 to 12 in. broad, 3- to 5-lobed, mature leaves light green and tending to be smooth above, paler and usually rusty-hairy beneath. Young leaves hairy on both surfaces, with conspicuous stipules at base of petioles. Fruit contained in bristly "button-balls" ¾ to 1¼ in. in diameter.

*Range:* South Coast Ranges to southern California and northward in the central valleys and the Sierra Nevada foothills to Tehama County, below 4,500 ft. February—April. Riparian Woodland.


## ROSE FAMILY (ROSACEAE)

**Mountain Mahogany** *(Cercocarpus ledifolius)*

Also known as Curl-leaf Mahogany. A small, evergreen tree or shrub 6 to 25 feet tall. Its short trunk is usually more or less crooked and its numerous stiff branches stand out in all directions producing a low, dense crown. It forms an important ground cover on dry windswept mountain slopes where few other species can survive. Its hard, dark, scaly bark is reddish-brown with a grayish tint. Wood is brownish-red and extremely hard. Due to the poor timber form of the tree, its has little value except for firewood and novelties.

*Leaves and fruit:* Leaves are thick and leathery, ½ to 1 in. long, ¼ in. wide, edges somewhat rolled under. Mature leaves dark green tending to be smooth above, paler and hairy beneath, margins entire, usually remaining on the tree for two seasons. Fruit small and dry with a long, hairy, and somewhat twisted tail.

*Range:* Dry, rocky slopes, Santa Rosa and San Jacinto Mountains, mountains on the western side of Mojave Desert north to Modoc and Siskiyou counties at elevations from 4,000 to 10,000 ft. April—May. Yellow Pine Forest, Sagebrush Scrub, Piñon—Juniper Woodland.

**Hard Tack** *(Cercocarpus betuloides)*

Also known as Birch-leaf Mahogany. A small evergreen tree or shrub 6 to 20 ft. tall, with more or less open and rounded crown. Bark on large trunks is thick, flaky, and reddish-brown; on large branches and small trunks it is smooth and dull gray to brownish. Its habitat and value are similar to those of the Mountain Mahogany.

*Leaves and fruit:* Leaves variable in shape, mostly obovate to oval, serrate above the middle, ½ to 1½ in. long, ½ to 1 in. wide, dark green and smooth above, paler and frequently hairy beneath. Straight parallel side veins. Flowers usually in clusters of twos or threes. Fruit dry, with long hairy flower tube on tail.

*Range:* Dry slopes and washes below 6,000 ft. of Coast Ranges and Sierra Nevada from Mexico to Oregon. March—May. Chaparral.

**Bitter Cherry** *(Prunus emarginata)*

A small deciduous tree 10 to 20 ft. tall, but may also occur as a shrub. Bark on mature trunks is smooth and dark brown. Tends to form dense chaparral cover on rocky and dampish slopes and canyons, checking rapid run off from heavy snow packs. The wood has little value except for fuel. Its fruit is eaten extensively by birds and many mammals.

*Leaves and fruit:* Leaves oblong-ovate to broadly elliptic, acute to obtuse, ¾ to 2½ in. long, ½ to 1 in. wide, with 1 to 4 glands near the base of leaf, finely serrate, dark green and smooth above, paler and sometimes slightly pubescent beneath. Flowers in short clusters of 3 to 10; fruit 1/3 to ½ in. in diameter, round, red to purplish-black, bitter.

*Range:* Widely distributed on mountain slopes and canyons from San Diego County north to British Columbia at elevations below 9,000 ft. April—May. Yellow Pine Forest, Chaparral.

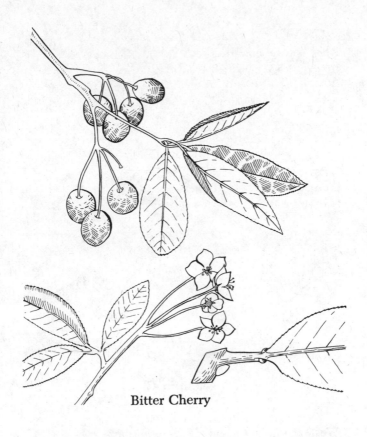

Bitter Cherry

**Desert Apricot** *(Prunus fremontii)*

A small deciduous tree or shrub 6 to 12 ft. tall. Its smooth reddish-brown twigs are often spine-tipped.

*Leaves and fruit:* Leaves roundish to broadly ovate ½ to 1 in. long, serrate, dark green above, paler beneath. Fruit yellowish and finely hairy. Stone has thick ridge on front side.

*Range:* Canyons below 4,000 ft. along western edge of Colorado desert from Palm Springs region to Baja California. February—March. Creosote Bush—Low Desert Scrub, Piñon—Juniper Woodland.

[ 81 ]

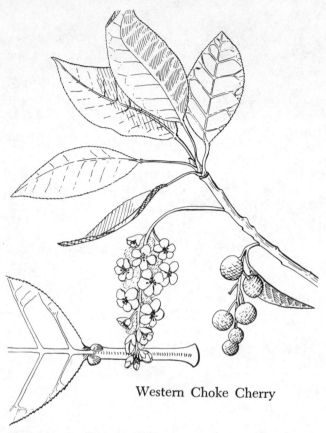

Western Choke Cherry

**Western Choke Cherry** *(Prunus virginiana)*

A small deciduous tree or shrub 6 to 20 ft. tall. New twigs are smooth or minutely hairy and greenish, turning light reddish-brown, with pointed, light brown leaf buds. Bark on trunks of mature trees is grayish-brown and somewhat scaly. Fruit is sweet when ripe but with an astringent aftertaste which probably accounts for the name "choke" cherry. It is frequently gathered and when cooked produces a rather delightful preserve. The fact that the fruit is greedily eaten by birds probably accounts for the wide distribution of this species.

*Leaves and fruit:* Leaves oblong to oblong-obovate, 1½ in. to 3½ in. long, ¾ to 1¾ in. wide, dark green and smooth above, slightly pubescent beneath, finely serrate, pointed at apex. One or two glands on leaf stalk near base of leaf. Flowers numerous, in racemes 3 to 6 in. long. Fruit roundish, about 1/3 in. in diameter, dark red to purple when ripe.

*Range:* Widely distributed in Coast Ranges and Sierra Nevada on dampish brushy slopes and flats from San Diego County to Washington at elevations below 8,200 ft. May—June. Southern Oak Woodland, Chaparral, Yellow Pine Forest.

### Hollyleaf Cherry *(Prunus ilicifolia)*

Also known as Islay. A small evergreen tree or shrub 6 to 25 ft. tall, with a thickly-branched crown and a short trunk. Reddish-brown bark of mature trunks is deeply furrowed and cut into small squarish divisions, while the bark of young twigs is smooth and varies from reddish-yellow to reddish-brown. It is extensively planted as an ornamental background tree or hedge. Its glossy foliage is widely used in making wreaths and other Christmas decorations. The Hollyleaf Cherry should not be confused with a closely related species, the Catalina Cherry, which may reach a height of 40 ft., with leaves which are also thick, leathery, and glossy but which are considerably larger and usually entire. Catalina Cherry is a native of the coastal islands and is extensively cultivated on the mainland. It hybridizes readily with the Hollyleaf Cherry and may occasionally escape and appear as a native.

*Leaves and fruit:* Leaves rather thick and leathery ovate to elliptic, 1 to 2 in. long, 1 to 1½ in. wide, dark green and glossy above, paler and yellowish beneath, usually spiny, occasionally almost entire. Fruit roundish, ½ to ¾ in. long, red to dark purple.

*Range:* Dry slopes and fans of the Coast Ranges and foothills from Napa County to Baja California at

[ 83 ]

elevations below 5,000 ft. April–May. Oak Woodland, Southern Oak Woodland, Chaparral.

**Toyon** *(Heteromeles arbutifolia)*

Also known as Christmas Berry. A small evergreen tree or shrub 10 to 20 ft. tall, with a much-branched crown and a relatively short trunk, its handsome green foliage and clusters of red berries lend much to the beauty of our California foothills in the autumn and early winter. It is extensively cultivated as an ornamental, although the variety *macrocarpa*, a native of Santa Catalina and San Clemente Islands, appears to be more desirable as an ornamental since its flower clusters are larger and its berry-like fruit reputed to be less appealing to birds.

*Leaves and fruit:* Leaves thick, leathery, oblong to elliptical, 2 to 4 in. long, 1 to 1¾ in. wide, smooth and glossy, dark green above, paler beneath, tending to be pointed at both ends, and rather sharply toothed. Fruit ovoid ¼ to 1/3 in. long, bright to pale red, berry-like.

*Range:* Common on brushy foothill slopes and canyons of the Coast Ranges from Humboldt County to Baja California and in the Sierra Nevada from Shasta County to Tulare County below 4,000 feet. June–July. Chaparral, Oak Woodland, Southern Oak Woodland.

## Pea Family (Leguminosae)

There are nine members of the Pea Family which attain tree size in southern California. All, with the exception of the Redbud and Smoke Tree, have pinnately compound leaves with numerous small leaflets producing a lacy effect when silhouetted against their native desert background. All produce pea-like flowers in racemes ranging in color from yellow to violet-purple. All, with the exception of the Redbud, can withstand the intense heat and drought of the desert, thereby providing shade and color for an otherwise bleak if ever-changing and fascinating landscape.

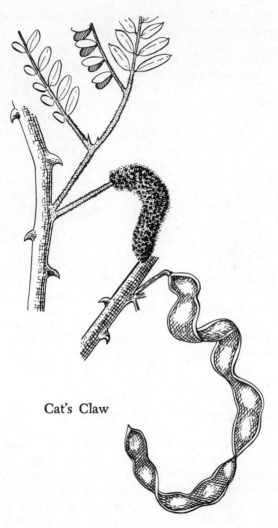

Cat's Claw

**Cat's Claw** *(Acacia greggii)*
This is a small deciduous tree 10 to 20 ft. tall with a much-branched crown and a short trunk. It occurs more frequently as a shrub. New light, reddish-brown

twigs are minutely hairy. Branches are armed with short, stout, curved, claw-like spines which account for its common name. The wood is hard, dense, and dull red. Due to the scarcity of sizable trees it has little or no commercial value other than for fence posts.

*Leaves, flowers, and fruit:* Gray-green leaves are bipinnate, 1 to 2 in. long, consisting of three pairs of primary leaflets or pinnae ½ to ¾ in. long, each of which has 4 to 6 pairs of smaller leaflets ⅛ to ¼ in. long; flowers yellow, in cylindrical spikes ½ to 1½ in. long; fruit a pod, compressed and somewhat constricted between each seed, 1 to 6 in. long and about ¾ in wide, containing 1 to 10 seeds.

*Range:* Colorado Desert and southern part of Mojave Desert; occasionally on desert side of southern California mountains. April–June. Creosote Bush–Low Desert Scrub, Piñon–Juniper Woodland.

### Honey Mesquite *(Prosopis glandulosa)*

This interesting denizen of the desert is a small, deciduous tree 10 to 20 ft. tall with many crooked branches and a short trunk. It may also occur as a much-branched shrub. The mesquite develops a huge, deep root system which makes it possible to survive severe drought conditions that would kill most other trees. Its reddish-brown wood is dense, close-grained, very hard, and heavy. It takes a beautiful polish. The small size and irregular shape of even the larger trees prevents the wood from having any extensive commercial importance, although locally it has some limited use in the production of novelties and certain types of furniture. Long fruit pods are very nutritious and are used by Indians and Mexicans for food. Flowers which bloom from April to June are the source of an excellent honey which accounts for the common name.

*Leaves, flowers, and fruit:* Smooth, bright green, bipinnate leaves consist of 2 or 3 pairs of primary leaflets or pinnae, 2½ to 4 in. long, each with 20 to 36 linear entire leaflets ½ to 1 in. long, with one or two thorns ¼ to 1½ in. long in axils of the leaves. Flowers greenish-yellow in slender spikes 2½ to 3 in. long; fruit pods linear, 3 to 8 in. long, curved, flattish, somewhat constricted between seeds.

*Range:* Colorado and Mojave deserts, upper San Joaquin Valley, Cuyama Valley, interior valleys of San Bernardino and San Diego counties to Lower California, and eastward to Texas. April—June. Creosote Bush—Low Desert Scrub, Southern Desert Wash, Desert Canal, Colorado River Bottom.

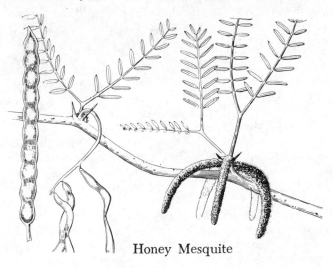

Honey Mesquite

**Screw-Bean Mesquite** *(Prosopis pubescens)*

This is a small tree or shrub 10 to 30 ft. tall with slender twigs and stout spines. Its physical characteristics and habitat are quite similar to those of the Honey Mesquite, except for its coiled seed pods, which, with the early spring growth, serve as food for livestock. Indians and Mexicans grind the ripe seeds into a meal which they use in making tortillas and other items of food.

*Leaves, flowers, and fruit:* Leaves pubescent, bipinnate, 1½ to 3 in. long, usually with two primary divisions, pinnae 1 to 2 in. long, each with 10 to 22 oblong leaflets, ⅛ to ⅜ in. long. Flowers yellowish, in spikes 2 to 3 in. long; fruit pods in clusters, sessile, coiled into a spring-like cylinder 1 to 1½ in. long.

*Range:* Colorado and Mojave deserts and western side of southern San Joaquin Valley. May—July. Creosote Bush—Low Desert Scrub, Southern Desert Wash, Colorado River Bottom, Desert Canal.

## Western Redbud *(Cercis occidentalis)*

Also known as California Redbud or Judas Tree. This is another of those small deciduous trees, 8 to 15 ft. tall, whose dense rounded crowns nearly reach the ground, making them appear like small green clumps on the hillside. The striking highly-colored pea-like flowers, which appear before the leaves in umbellate clusters along the branches, make the Western Redbud one of our most attractive native flowering trees or shrubs. It is extensively cultivated in parks and gardens throughout the West.

*Leaves, flowers, and fruit:* Leaves entire, smooth, glossy, almost round in outline, sometimes slightly notched at apex, heart-shaped at base and somewhat palmately veined. Flowers deep reddish-pink to reddish-purple, only rarely white; fruit pods 1½ to 3 in. long, turning dull red when mature.

*Range:* Desert slopes and canyons of Laguna and Cuyamaca Mountains in southern California. More widely distributed in the inner Coast Ranges and Sierra Nevada foothills of central and northern California. February—April. Riparian Woodlands, Chaparral, Southern Oak Woodland.

**Horse-Bean** *(Parkinsonia aculeata)*

Also known as Mexican Palo Verde or Jerusalem-Thorn. An interesting small desert tree 15 to 30 ft. tall with sparse gray-green foliage and spines ½ to 1 in. long at the bases of its leaf clusters. Grazing animals browse extensively upon its new twigs. It is widely planted in southern California desert towns, primarily because of its ability to survive in hot, dry areas. It has become naturalized in some areas.

*Leaves, flowers, and fruit:* Bipinnate leaves attached to a very short petiole, each pinna or leaf-stalk 6 to 18 in. long, bearing 40 to 60 flattened gray-green ovate to obovate leaflets, each about ⅛ in. long. Leaves drop early. Fragrant yellow flowers ½ to ¾ in. wide form erect racemes 3 to 6 in. long; fruit pods 3 to 6 in. long, restricted between seeds and conspicuously striped logitudinally.

*Range:* Common in Arizona and Mexico, reported in the lower Colorado River valley. June—August. Desert Urban, Desert Rural.

**Little Leaf Horse-Bean** *(Cercidium microphyllum)*

A small tree or shrub 5 to 25 ft. tall with yellowish-green bark and stiff spine-tipped branchlets.

*Leaves, flowers, and fruit:* Pubescent leaves bipinnate, with one or sometimes two pairs of pinnae from a very short or almost sessile petiole. Each pinna ½ to 1½ in. long, with 4 to 8 pairs of minute, elliptic, entire leaflets about 1/16 in. long, which fall shortly after reaching maturity. Flowers pale yellow in loose racemes about 1 in. long; fruit pod linear-cylindrical constricted between seeds, 1 to 3 in. long, 1 to 4 seeds.

*Range:* Whipple Mountains of San Bernardino County, Arizona, and Mexico. April—May. Creosote Bush—Low Desert Scrub.

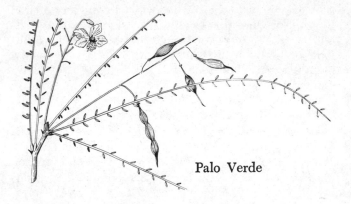

Palo Verde

### Palo Verde *(Cercidium floridum)*

Also known as Green Bark Acacia. A small tree or large shrub 15 to 35 ft. tall. Bark of all limbs and trunks of young trees is a light-yellowish- to bluish-green, which offers a pleasing contrast to the otherwise parched desert scenery. Bark on the trunk of mature trees is light brown with a reddish tinge. It is leafless during most of the year. Pods are harvested by the native Indians for food.

*Leaves, flowers, and fruit:* Leaves are bipinnate, alternate, 2, rarely 4 or 6, pinnae about 1 in. long, with 2 to 4 pairs of oblong leaflets ⅛ to ⅜ in. long, attached to a short petiole. Yellow flowers ½ to ¾ in. wide in axillary racemes 2 to 4 in. long; oblong fruit pods 2 to 4 in. long, 1 to. 8 seeded, somewhat constricted.

*Range:* Colorado Desert, east to Arizona and south to Lower California and mainland Mexico. March–May. Creosote Bush–Low Desert Scrub, Southern Desert Wash.

### Smoke Tree *(Dalea spinosa)*

Also known as Indigo Bush. A much-branched and nearly leafless small tree or shrub, 6 to 25 ft. tall, with

[ 90 ]

yellowish-green or ashy-gray spiny branchlets. These are closely covered with fine grayish-white or hoary hairs and dotted with glands, giving the tree a smoky appearance and producing a never-to-be-forgotten impression. It has been the motif for many famous desert paintings. Hundreds of feet of colored film have been exposed in the attempt to record its subtle charm.

*Leaves, flowers, and fruit:* Leaves few, simple, alternate, linear, oblong to spatula-shaped, ¼ to 1 in. long, 1/16 to ⅛ in. wide, almost sessile, early deciduous, Flowers dark blue to violet-purple, hence the name "Indigo Bush," ⅛ to ½ in. long in short spike-like racemes ½ to 1 in. long; fruit pods, covered with grayish-white or hoary fine hairs, ¼ to ½ in. long with 1 or 2 seeds.

*Range:* Colorado Desert east to Arizona and south to Mexico. June—July. Creosote Bush—Low Desert Scrub, Southern Desert Wash.

## Desert Ironwood *(Olneya tesota)*

This is a small, stocky, spiny tree 15 to 25 ft. tall, the trunk of which may attain a diameter of 6 or more in. The bark is thin, deep reddish-brown, and flaky. Wood is heavy, hard, deep chocolate-brown mottled with red and surrounded with a very narrow band of lemon-yellow sapwood. It is armed with stout curved spines ⅛ to 1/3 in. long, which occur in pairs at the base of the leaves.

*Leaves, flowers, and fruits:* Leaves grayish-green covered with a dense coat of hoary, fine hairs; pinnately compound, each leaf consisting of 8 to 24 oblong wedge-shaped, entire and sessile leaflets ¼ to ½ in. long. Flowers pea-like, violet-purple, in axillary racemes; pod 1 to 2 in. long, constricted between seeds, 1 to 8 black seeds.

*Range:* Southern Colorado Desert east to Arizona and south to Mexico. Creosote Bush—Low Desert Scrub, Southern Desert Wash.

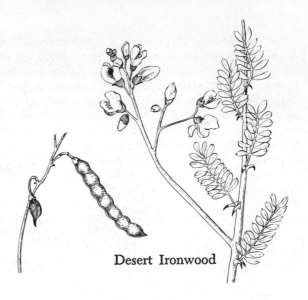

Desert Ironwood

## Cacao Family (Sterculiaceae)
### flannel bush (fremontodendron)

There are two species and several sub-species of these colorful plants which are native to California. They are sometimes called "slippery elm" due to their mucilaginous bark and occasionally are also known as "silver oak" because of the light-colored under surface of their leaves. However, they are commonly known in the nursery trade as fremontia or flannel bush and are extensively cultivated in gardens and parks due to their long and showy blooming season. The showy part of the flower is the calyx, which consists of five petal-like sepals, each with a hairy gland at the base. They thrive best where there is good drainage.

### Mexican Flannel Bush
#### *(Fremontodendron mexicana)*

This is small evergreen tree or shrub 8 to 20 ft. tall, whose new branches are covered with a mass of dense star-shaped mats of woolly hairs which later turn brown.

*Leaves, flowers, and fruits:* Leaves simple, alternate, thickish, shallowly palmately 5 to 7 lobed, sparsely star-shaped pubescent above, densely covered with tawny and matted woolly hairs beneath. Flowers consist of a somewhat bell-shaped orange calyx 2½ to 3½ in. across which tends to become somewhat reddish on the outside near the base; fruit dark-colored seeds in densely hairy 4- or 5-valved capsule.

*Range:* Otay and Jamul Mountains, San Diego County adjacent to Lower California. March—June. Chaparral, Southern Oak Woodland.

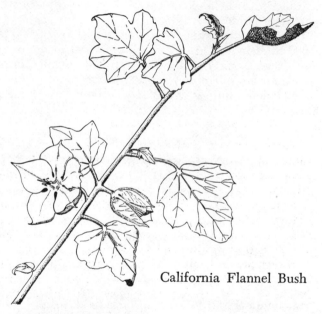

California Flannel Bush

### California Flannel Bush
*(Fremontodendron californica)*

A small evergreen tree or shrub 10 to 20 ft. tall with a short trunk and open crown of spreading branches. Frequently as a shrub it tends to form dense thickets with other foothill chapparal, producing a protective cover on dry, rocky foothill slopes. Range cattle and deer browse upon its new twigs. It blooms more profusely and during a shorter time than the Mexican Flannel Bush.

*Leaves and fruit:* Leaves simple, alternate, broadly round-ovate, usually 3 to 5 palmate, lobes rarely entire, dull green and sparsely star-shaped pubescent above, densely covered with tawny and matted woolly hairs beneath. Flowers consist of a flat, clear yellow calyx 1½ to 2½ in. in diameter. Fruit is an ovoid capsule ¾ to 1 in. long covered with dense bristly persistent hairs.

*Range:* Lower granite and limestone slopes, 3,000 to 6,000 ft. of inner Coast Range from Shasta County to San Diego County and the western side of the Sierra Nevada from Mariposa County to Kern County. May—June. Piñon—Juniper Woodland, Yellow Pine Forest, Chaparral.

## MAPLE FAMILY (ACERACEAE)

In southern California we find three of the four maples which are native to the state. We also find a great many introduced varieties in our parks, streets, and gardens, many of which are very ornamental and more desirable as domestics than our native varieties. All maples have opposite, deciduous, and simple-lobed leaves, except the Box Elder which has compound leaves. The fruit of all maples is a double samara with terminal wings.

### Mountain Maple *(Acer glabrum* var. *diffusum)*
This is a small tree or shrub 6 to 20 ft. tall with greenish-white twigs, in contrast to the Mountain Maple of northern California which usually has reddish twigs.

*Leaves and fruit:* Leaf blades smooth, shiny above and pale green beneath, ¾ to 1½ in. long, ¾ to 2 in.

wide, palmately 3-lobed, occasionally with two supplementary lobes at the base.

*Range:* San Jacinto and San Bernardino Mountains at elevations of 6,500 to 9,000 ft. April—June. Yellow Pine Forest, Lodgepole Pine—White Fir Forest.

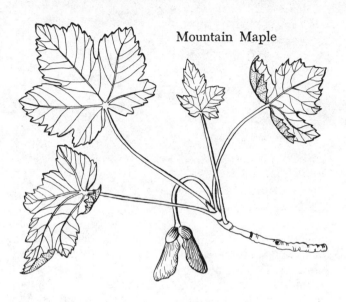

Mountain Maple

**Big Leaf Maple** *(Acer macrophyllum)*

Variously known as Oregon Maple, Canyon Maple, Water Maple or White Maple. This maple is a tall, broad-crowned tree 30 to 100 ft. tall which may attain a trunk diameter of 12 to 20 in. It is somewhat smaller in most of southern California. Bark of mature trees is rough with hard, scaly ridges that vary in color from pale grayish to dull reddish-brown. The wood is fine-grained, hard, firm, and of good commercial quality. It is an important lumber tree in certain parts of the Pacific area where hardwoods are scarce. It is easily recognized by its large 3 to 5 palm-

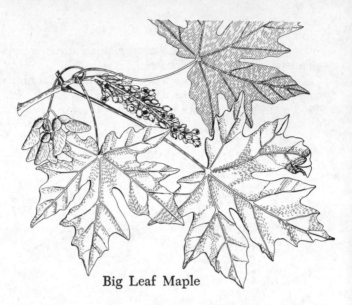

Big Leaf Maple

ately-lobed leaves, which vary greatly in size depending on light, moisture, and soil conditions.

*Leaves and fruit:* Leaf blades vary from 6 to 18 in. long and as wide, shiny dark green above, paler and somewhat pubescent beneath, deeply-lobed, with lobes which may be 2- to 4-toothed or almost entire, petioles 6 to 12 in. long. Samaras or winged fruits vary in size, wings 1 to 2 inches long, early glabrous, seed body densely covered with short hairs.

*Range:* San Bernardino Mountains to British Columbia on moist slopes below 5,000 ft. April—May. Riparian Woodland, many plant communities.

**Box Elder** *(Acer negundo)*

This is a fast-growing tree 20 to 60 ft. tall with a short clear trunk and a broad, roundish crown. Its bark is grayish-brown with regular and deep furrows. New twigs are slender, greenish, and pubescent. It is the only native member of the Maple family which has compound leaves. The Box Elder was extensively planted by the early settlers to provide shade and windbreak. However, it has proven to be a rather undesirable domestic tree due to several objectionable characteristics: it is what some landscape designers call a "dirty" tree. It is brittle and frequently drops branches during a storm, its heavy crop of samaras drop over a long period of time, it serves as a host to the highly objectionable Box-elder Bug, and it drops its leaves early and continues to do so for months. The sap was reputedly used by the Indians and early settlers as a source of maple sugar.

*Leaves and fruit:* Leaves pinnately compound, 3 or rarely 5 leaflets, each leaflet more or less lobed or deeply serrate, 2 to 4 in. long, bright green and nearly smooth above, paler and pubescent beneath, samaras abundant, usually finely pubescent.

*Range:* Stream banks and valley bottoms in Coast Ranges and Sierra Nevada foothills below 6,000 ft., infrequent on southern slopes of San Bernardino and San Jacinto Mountains. March–April. Riparian Woodland, many plant communities.

Box Elder

California Buckeye

## BUCKEYE FAMILY (HIPPOCASTANACEAE)

**California Buckeye** *(Aesculus californica)*

Also known as Horse Chestnut or California Pear. A small deciduous tree 15 to 30 ft. tall with a broad round crown and a smooth gray bark. It is one of California's most unusual and picturesque trees. In the early spring we see its profuse and beautiful large white flower clusters and lush green foliage silhouetted against the dry and rolling foothills. With the advent of early summer drought its leaves begin to turn brown and by midsummer these same hillsides are dotted with what looks like a collection of dead or dying trees. Soon thereafter they lose their leaves and display their large pear-shaped fruit and shiny, smoky-gray branches to await the early autumn rains so as to start the cycle all over again.

*Leaves and fruit:* Leaves dark green above, paler beneath, nearly smooth to finely pubescent, opposite, palmately compound with 5 to 7 oblong lanceolate serrate leaflets, 3 to 6 in. long, 1½ to 2 in. wide. Flowers ill-scented, pinkish-white with orange anthers in large erect cylindrical clusters 6 to 10 in. long; fruit a smooth pear-shaped pod, usually containing 1, sometimes 2, glossy seeds, 1 to ¾ in. in diameter. Seeds bitter and slightly toxic.

*Range:* Dry slopes and canyons of Sierra Nevada and Coast Range from Siskiyou and Shasta counties south to Los Angeles County below 4,000 ft. May—June. Southern Oak Woodland.

## Dogwood Family (Cornaceae)

**Mountain Dogwood** *(Cornus nuttallii)*

A small deciduous tree 10 to 40 ft. tall which varies greatly in form from a rounded to a narrow, long, open crown. Trunks are usually long and clean, with smooth, thin, ashy-brown or reddish bark. Young twigs vary from green to dark red. It is another of our spectacular native trees whose large white to pinkish flowers lend so much to the beauty of our mountain woods and meadows in the early spring. Its spring charm can only be surpassed by the brilliance of its autumn coloration, due to clusters of bright red fruit and its red and orange foliage.

*Leaves and fruit:* Leaves are simple, opposite, deciduous, narrow, elliptic to obovate, or even ovate to almost round, 3 to 5 in. long, 1½ to 3 in. wide, bright green and slightly hairy above, paler and pubescent to smooth beneath. Flowers small, yellowish-green, crowded into a compact head, surrounded by usually 6, sometimes 4 or 5, conspicuous white bracts sometimes tinted with green or pink. Fruit a dense cluster of red to scarlet drupes about ½ in. long.

*Range:* Coastal mountains from British Columbia to southern California and western slope of Sierra Nevada below 6,000 ft. April—July. Riparian Woodland, Yellow Pine Forest, Broadleaf Evergreen Forest.

[ 99 ]

### Madrone *(Arbutus menziesii)*

This is a handsome widely-branched evergreen tree 20 to 125 ft. tall (smaller in the southern part of its range) with a polished terra-cotta colored bark which usually appears under a fully scaling dark brown and fissured older bark. The madrone is a picturesque tree which lends much to the beauty of some of our slightly humid hillsides and canyons. The attractiveness of the Madrone is due not only to the color of its bark and its beautiful, glossy, dark green leaves, but also to the large clusters of urn-shaped white flowers and brilliant orange-red berry-like fruit which ripen in the late fall and make a very colorful display. It is quite extensively cultivated as a garden or park tree.

*Leaves, flowers, and fruit:* Leaves dark green and glossy above, paler beneath, thick and leathery, narrowly elliptic to somewhat ovate, 3 to 6 in. long, 1¾ to 2¾ in. wide, entire or finely serrate. Flowers urn-shaped, about ¼ in. long, in large clusters, white to pinkish. Fruit 1/3 to ½ in. in diameter, somewhat fleshy, frequently abundant, deep orange to red.

*Range:* Foothills and mountain slopes below 5,000 ft. in Coast Ranges from British Columbia to Baja California, most abundant from San Luis Obispo County to Del Norte County and in the Sierra Nevada from Mariposa County to Shasta County. March–May. Southern Oak Woodland, Broadleaf Evergreen Forest, Redwood Forest.

### Bigberry Manzanita *(Arctostaphylos glauca)*

This is a small, picturesque, evergreen tree or shrub 8 to 25 ft. tall with a smooth reddish-brown trunk. Twigs are greenish and either smooth or finely hairy. It is the only manzanita in southern California that normally attains tree proportions. The fruit of the manzanita, "little apples," which are really berry-like drupes, were very important in the diet of the early California Indians. Some authorities consider that the manzanita was as important a source of food for the early Indians as the oaks or nut pines. The wood is extremely hard and was used by the Indians in making certain utensils and trinkets. In recent years the manzanita has been badly exploited by commercial agencies and souvenir hunters because of the fascinating asymmetry of its branches and the richly skin-tight bark, which make it an attractive collector's item. Unless this wanton practice is discouraged we may eventually lose not only one of the picturesque aspects of our dry mountain slopes but also a very important erosion retardant.

*Leaves, flowers, and fruit:* Leaves 1 to 1¾ in. long, ½ to 1 in. wide, pale greenish on both surfaces, petioles ¼ to ½ in. long, stomates on both surfaces. Flowers about ½ in. long, white or tinged with pink. Fruit about ½ in. long and very sticky; nutlets united into a solid stone.

*Range:* Coast and inner Coast Ranges of southern California. December—March. Chaparral, Joshua Tree —High Desert Woodland.

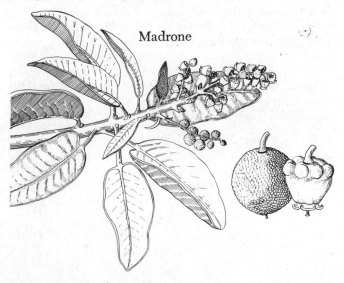

Madrone

# Olive Family (Oleaceae)
## ash (fraxinus)

There are three members of the ash genus found in southern California, all of which are small trees or tree-like shrubs. They have deciduous pinnately compound leaves except for the small Dwarf Ash whose leaves are usually simple, but which may also occasionally have compound leaves with 2 or 3 leaflets. Fruit is a single-seeded samara. None of the southern California ashes should be confused with the larger Oregon Ash which is found in the Coast Range from Santa Clara County to British Columbia and in the Sierra Nevada from Kern County to Modoc County.

### Flowering Ash *(Fraxinus dipetala)*

Also known as Foothill Ash or Mountain Ash. A small deciduous tree or tree-like shrub 6 to 18 ft. tall whose young branchlets tend to be 4-angled, slender, and somewhat pubescent. Older branches become smooth.

*Leaves, flowers, and fruit:* Leaves opposite, pinnately compound, 2½ to 6 in. long, leaflets usually 3 to 9, thin, smooth on both surfaces, serrate, sometimes entire below middle, ovate to obovate, ½ to 1½ in. long, ⅜ to ¾ inches wide. Fruit a single samara ¾ to 1 in. long, winged along the sides, often notched at the tip. Conspicuous part of flower consists of two showy white petals.

*Range:* Dry slopes inner South Coast Range and San Bernardino Mountains, also Sierra Nevada foothills from Shasta County south. April—May. Southern Oak Woodland, Chaparral.

### Arizona Ash *(Fraxinus velutina)*

A small deciduous tree 15 to 30 ft. tall which usually has a rather short and slender trunk, with grayish, sometimes faintly reddish, soft and scaly bark. Crowns of the larger trees are dense and quite symmetrical.

Flowering Ash

New branchlets are round, usually reddish and smooth, but sometimes dull grayish and occasionally covered with fine woolly hairs.

*Leaves, flowers, and fruit:* Leaves opposite, pinnately compound, 4 to 6 in. long, 3 to 7 leaflets; leaflets lanceolate to ovate, 1 to 1½ in. long, thickish pale green and smooth above, paler and hairy beneath, finely serrate above the middle. Fruit a single samara about 1 inch long, with terminal wing; flowers greenish without petals.

*Range:* Canyons and stream banks below 5,000 ft., Los Angeles County to San Diego County, desert mountain slopes north to Owens Lake. March—April. Riparian Woodland, Yellow Pine Forest, Southern Oak Woodland, Chaparral.

### Dwarf Ash *(Fraxinus anomala)*

Also known as Singleleaf Ash. A small, bushy deciduous tree or tree-like shrub 15 to 20 ft. tall. Its branchlets are smooth or somewhat hairy and tend to be 4 angled. Leaves usually reduced to a single leaf blade or leaflet, although it may sometimes have 3-pinnately compound leaflets. This characteristic tends to distinguish it from the Arizona Ash.

*Leaves, flowers, and fruit:* Leaves simple or pinnately compound. Leaflets broadly ovate to almost round, 1 to 2 in. long, 1 to 2 in. wide, dark green and smooth above, paler beneath, entire or very slightly rounded and serrate. Fruit samara, ½ to ¾ in. long with a rounded wing. Flowers greenish without petals.

*Range:* Mojave Desert and dry canyons eastward to Colorado. April—May. Piñon—Juniper Woodland.

## BIGNONIA FAMILY (BIGNONIACAE)

### Desert Willow *(Chilopsis linearis)*

A small, usually slender deciduous tree or shrub 10 to 20 ft. tall. Its branchlets are very slender, usually smooth, sometimes minutely hairy, and vary in color from yellowish to reddish-brown. It is not a member of the Willow family; however, because of its habitat and its long, narrow, willow-like leaves it has come to be known as "Desert Willow."

*Leaves, flowers, and fruit:* Leaves yellow-green 4 to 6 in. long, sometimes longer, ⅛ to ¼ in. wide, smooth entire, sessile, linear or lanceolate or often sickle-shaped, usually opposite on lower part of twig, alternate or whorled near end of twig. Fruit a long linear capsule 6 to 12 in. long with many oblong, thin, hairy winged seeds. Flowers 1 to 2 in. long, showy, pink to whitish with purplish markings and yellow patches in the throat, borne in short terminal clusters.

*Range:* Washes and stream beds of southern California desert areas east- and southward. May—September. Joshua Tree—High Desert Woodland, Creosote Bush—Low Desert Scrub, Southern Desert Wash.

Desert Willow

There are three species of elderberries which attain tree size in California, two of which, Blue Elderberry and Mexican Elderberry, are found in southern California, the Red Elderberry is found north of our region. The fruit of elderberries is used for making various drinks and preserves. The elderberry also appears prominently in some of our early Indian mythology.

**Blue Elderberry** *(Sambucus caerulea)*

A small, deciduous tree or shrub 20 ft. tall. Its branches have a large soft, pithy center. The bark of mature trunks is thin and dark yellowish-brown. New twigs are usually smooth, sparsely hairy at first, then shiny reddish-brown and somewhat angular.

*Leaves, flowers, and fruit:* Leaves opposite, pinnately compound, 5 to 7 in. long or even longer on new vigorous shoots. Leaflets 5 to 9, 1 to 4 in. long, oblong-lanceolate to ovate, smooth and yellow-green above, lighter and smooth to hairy beneath, serrate except near apex, sessile or very short-stalked, frequently with uneven base, lower leaflets occasionally pinnately divided. Flowers small, white in flat-topped clusters, 4 to 8 in. wide. Fruit spherical about ¼ in. in diameter, dark bluish with whitish bloom.

*Range:* Open woods, moist flats, and stream banks of upper middle to lower elevations in Coast Ranges from San Diego County to British Columbia and in Sierra Nevada. June–September. Yellow Pine Forest, Riparian Woodland.

**Mexican Elderberry** *(Sambucus mexicana)*

A small deciduous tree or shrub 6 to 20 ft. tall, quite similar to the Blue Elderberry, but somewhat more restricted in its habitat.

*Leaves, flowers, and fruit:* Leaves opposite, pinnately compound, 5 to 7 in. long. Leaflets 5 to 9, 2 to 5 in. long, 1 to 2 in. wide, usually thick and leathery, lanceolate, soft-pubescent above and below, serrate except at apex. Lower leaflets sometimes divided. Flowers pale yellow, fragrant, in flat-topped clusters 6 to 10 in. wide. Fruit spherical, about ⅛ in. in diameter, dark blue to almost black with pale whitish bloom, large clusters.

*Range:* Open flats, valleys and canyons below 4,500 ft. from Lake and Glenn counties to Baja California and east to Arizona. Southern Oak Woodland.

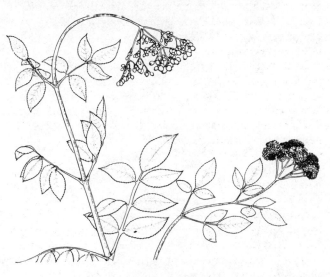

Mexican Elderberry

Point
Lobos

MONTEREY

Big Sur

COAST RANGE

SANTA LUCIA RANGE

SOUTHERN
CALIFORNIA

WHITE MTS.

INYO M.

SAN
LUIS
OBISPO

San Luis Obispo

Bakersfield

KERN

TEHACHAPI MTS.

Cuyama R.

SANTA
BARBARA

SAN
RAFAEL
MTS.

Santa Ynez R.

VENTURA

Santa Clara R.

SAN
GABRIEL
MTS.

SANTA

Santa Barbara

MONICA
MTS.

LOS
ANGEL

Los Angeles

ORANG

P

A

C

I

F

I

C

O

C

E

A

N

Santa Rosa I.

Santa Cruz I.

N

W

E

S

San Nicolas I.

Santa Catalina I.

San Clemente I.

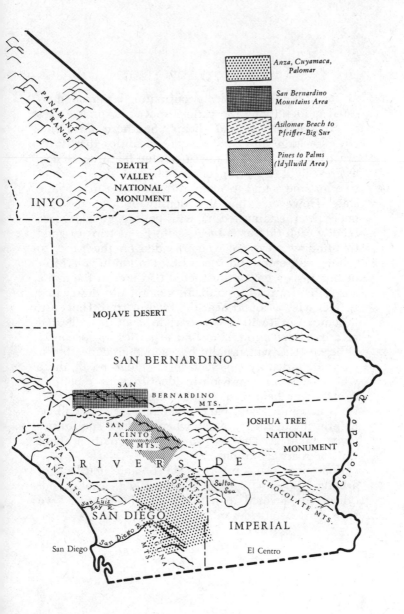

Anza, Cuyamaca, Palomar

San Bernardino Mountains Area

Asilomar Beach to Pfeiffer-Big Sur

Pines to Palms (Idyllwild Area)

PANAMINT RANGE

DEATH VALLEY NATIONAL MONUMENT

INYO

MOJAVE DESERT

SAN BERNARDINO

SAN BERNARDINO MTS.

SAN JACINTO MTS.

JOSHUA TREE NATIONAL MONUMENT

SANTA ANA MTS.

R I V E R S I D E

San Luis Rey R.

SAN DIEGO

San Diego R.

LAGUNA MTS.

SANTA ROSA MTS.

Salton Sea

CHOCOLATE MTS.

Colorado R.

IMPERIAL

San Diego

El Centro

[ 109 ]

# WHERE TO SEE TREES

One of the first problems confronting a person interested in identifying the various species of native trees is "Where do we find them?" Southern California covers a large area and includes localities that differ greatly in climatic and physiographic features. Hence, as one might expect, specimens of a certain species of tree may be found in many different localities of the state. However, when the identity of a species has once been established it will be recognized more readily each time it is seen again. Field trips to good tree-finding areas are recommended on the pages to follow with maps and species lists to guide you. Most of the areas are quite restricted and are, in the main, accessible by road or trail. In general the designated species will be found near the road or trail. However, in some cases it will be necessary to scout the indicated area carefully in order to find a particular specimen. Other species will usually be encountered nearby or en route. Identify all new species and recall those which have been previously identified, as repetition is extremely helpful in fixing recognizable characteristics in mind. Local park and forest rangers will be helpful in suggesting areas where certain species are to be found, as well as providing information about trail or road conditions.

You may also find trees in botanic gardens or arboretums. Some specialize primarily in exotics, but others are devoted to native California plants. Two such gardens are described here.

# MAP I

## NATIVE TREES FOUND IN THE
## PINES TO PALMS—IDYLLWILD AREA

A. Trees along or near Highways 4 and 111 from Cranston Station to Palm Springs. Numerals indicate locations on the map.

I. Cranston Station up stream along Highway 74 and the San Jacinto River bottom for a distance of about seven miles. Specimens are scattered.

| | |
|---|---|
| Fremont Cottonwood | Engelmann Oak |
| Red Willow | Blue Elderberry |
| Sandbar Willow | Toyon |
| Arroyo Willow | Western Sycamore |
| White Alder | Big Cone Spruce |
| Coast Live Oak | Incense Cedar |
| Canyon Live Oak | Mojave Yucca |

II. Mountain Center Area from two miles west of Mountain Center to Hemet Reservoir on Highway 74, also two miles on road from Mountain Center towards Idyllwild. Specimens are scattered.

| | |
|---|---|
| Big Cone Spruce | Oracle Oak |
| Incense Cedar | California Black Oak |
| Western Yellow Pine | Canyon Live Oak |
| Jeffrey Pine | Interior Live Oak |
| Coulter Pine | Arroyo Willow |
| Fremont Cottonwood | Red Willow |
| White Alder | Blue Elderberry |

III. Idyllwild Area, both sides of Strawberry Creek from Inspiration Point and below Idyllwild Arts Foundation, through Idyllwild and Fern Valley to Tahquitz Creek crossing. Specimens are scattered.

[ 111 ]

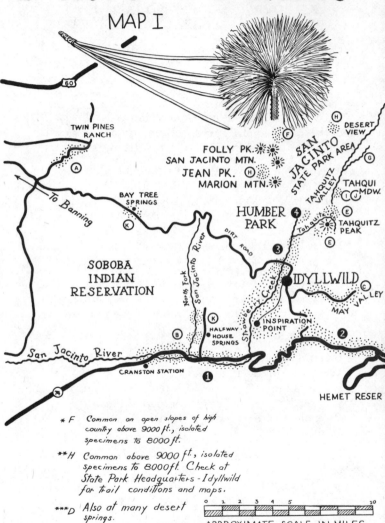

# Pines to Palms

## MAP I

60

TWIN PINES
RANCH

Ⓐ

To Banning

BAY TREE
SPRINGS

Ⓚ

Ⓕ

FOLLY PK.⁂
SAN JACINTO MTN.
JEAN PK. Ⓗ
MARION MTN.⁂

SAN
JACINTO
STATE PARK AREA

Ⓗ DESERT
VIEW

Ⓖ

Tahquitz Valley

TAHQUI
Ⓒ MDW.

Ⓔ

Ⓔ TAHQUITZ
PEAK

Ⓔ

HUMBER
PARK ⓸

⓷

IDYLLWILD

Ⓒ

MAY VALLEY

SOBOBA
INDIAN
RESERVATION

North Fork
San Jacinto River

Tahquitz

Strawberry Creek

DIRT ROAD

Ⓑ

Ⓚ

HALFWAY
HOUSE
SPRINGS

INSPIRATION
POINT

⓶

San Jacinto River

CRANSTON STATION

Ⓝ

Ⓐ

HEMET RESER.

* F  Common on open slopes of high
country above 9000 ft., isolated
specimens to 8000 ft.

**H  Common above 9000 ft., isolated
specimens to 8000ft. Check at
State Park Headquarters-Idyllwild
for trail conditions and maps.

***D  Also at many desert
springs.

```
0   1   2   3   4   5              10
```
APPROXIMATE SCALE IN MILES

[ 112 ]

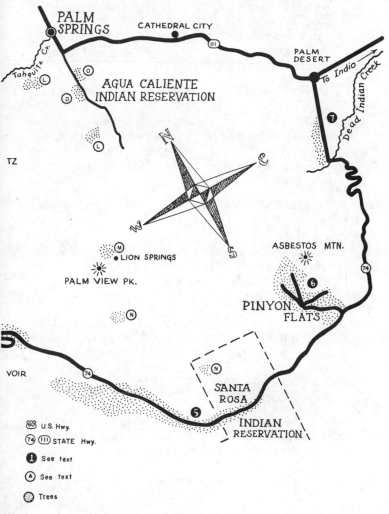

| | |
|---|---|
| Fremont Cottonwood | Canyon Live Oak |
| Black Cottonwood | Hard Tack |
| Golden Willow | White Fir |
| Arroyo Willow | Incense Cedar |
| White Alder | Western Yellow Pine |
| Mountain Dogwood | Jeffrey Pine |
| Blue Elderberry | Coulter Pine |
| California Black Oak | Sugar Pine |
| Oracle Oak | Bigberry Manzanita |
| Interior Live Oak | |

IV. Humber Park Area.—specimens are concentrated.

| | |
|---|---|
| White Fir | Coulter Pine |
| Incense Cedar | California Black Oak |
| Sugar Pine | Canyon Live Oak |
| Western Yellow Pine | Bigberry Manzanita |
| Jeffrey Pine | |

V. Hillsides from Kenworthy Station to eastern boundary of Santa Rosa Indian Reservation on Highway 4

Palmer Oak in thickets on both sides of highway. Isolated specimens of Parry Pine on or near highway, numerous on Vanderventer Flat.

| | |
|---|---|
| Blue Elderberry | Jeffrey Pine |
| Coast Live Oak | |

VI. Piñon Flats, north and south of Alpine Village on Highway 74 and the Piñon Flats Area. Specimens are concentrated.

| | |
|---|---|
| One Leaf Piñon Pine | California Juniper |
| Mojave Yucca | |

VII. The flat area, at the base of the grade, in the drainage basin of Dead Indian Creek, about three miles south of Palm Desert. Specimens are scattered.

Smoke Tree
Palo Verde

B. Native trees to be found along or near secondary roads or trails within the area included in the Pines to Palms Map. There are thirty miles of good trails in the Mount Jacinto Wild Area. Check location and conditions of trails at Ranger Headquarters. Letters indicate locations on the map.

| | |
|---|---|
| A | Arizona Ash |
| B | Engelmann Oak |
| C | Interior Live Oak |
| D | California Fan Palm |
| E | Mountain Mahogany |
| F | Limber Pine |
| G | Nuttall Willow |
| H | Lodgepole Pine |
| I | Watson's Willow |
| J | Bitter Cherry |
| K | California Laurel |
| L, | Catsclaw |
| M | Big Leaf Maple |
| N | Box Elder |
| O | Desert Willow |

## MAP II

### NATIVE TREES FOUND IN THE ANZA–CUYAMACA–PALOMAR AREA

(1) Anza–Borrego Desert State Park
This large and fascinating desert area contains nearly one-half-million acres in which is found a wide variety of characteristic flora including the following native trees. Since the area is large, with few trails, it is advisable to check with the rangers at Park Headquarters before undertaking a search for trees located in out-of-the-way areas. A visit to this interesting area will be rewarding. The park is traversed by Highway

78 east from Julian or west from junction of Highways
78 and 99 near the southern end of Salton Sea.

One Leaf Piñon Pine　　Smoke Tree
Coulter Pine　　　　　Desert Ironwood
California Juniper　　　Western Sycamore
Desert Willow　　　　White Alder
Desert Apricot　　　　California Black Oak
Hollyleaf Cherry　　　Coast Live Oak
Catsclaw　　　　　　Canyon Live Oak
Honey Mesquite　　　Fremont Cottonwood
Screw-bean Mesquite　Willows
Western Redbud　　　Blue Elderberry
Palo Verde　　　　　Mojave Yucca

(2) Cuyamaca Rancho State Park

Sugar Pine (A) (B)　　　Western Sycamore (C)
Western Yellow Pine (A)　White Alder (C)
Jeffrey Pine (C)　　　　Fremont Cottonwood (C)
Coulter Pine (C)　　　　Cuyamaca Cypress (B)
White Fir (B)　　　　　Blue Elderberry (C)
Incense Cedar (C)　　　Red Willow (C)
Canyon Live Oak (C)　　Arroyo Willow (C)
Coast Live Oak (C)　　　Western Choke
California Black Oak (C)　　Cherry (C)

(3) Palomar Mountain Area

White Fir (A)　　　　　Blue Oak (A)
Big Cone Spruce (A)　　White Alder (A)
Incense Cedar (A)　　　Fremont Cottonwood (A)
Coulter Pine (A)　　　　Blue Elderberry (A)
Knobcone Pine (A)　　　Western Sycamore (A)
Engelmann Oak (A)　　Mountain Mahogany (A)
Canyon Live Oak (A)　　Red Willow (A)
Coast Live Oak (A)　　　Arroyo Willow (A)
California Black Oak (A)

# Anza Cuyamaca Palomar

## MAP II

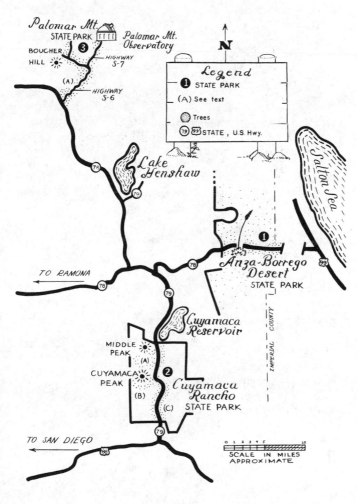

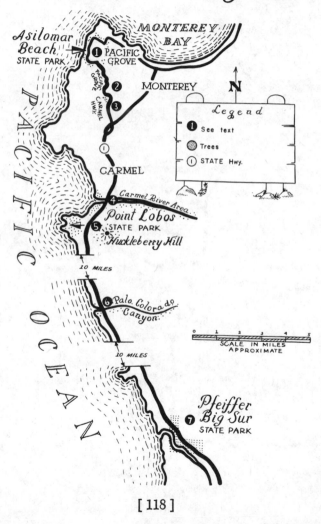

# Asilomar Beach to Pfeiffer Big Sur
## MAP III

MONTEREY BAY

Asilomar Beach STATE PARK

❶ PACIFIC GROVE

PACIFIC GROVE CARMEL HWY.

❷

❸

MONTEREY

Ⓝ

PACIFIC

①

CARMEL

Carmel River Area

❹

Point Lobos STATE PARK

❺

Huckleberry Hill

OCEAN

10 MILES

❻ Palo Colorado Canyon

10 MILES

Legend

❶ See text

Trees

① STATE Hwy.

0 1 2 3 4 5
SCALE IN MILES
APPROXIMATE

Pfeiffer Big Sur
❼ STATE PARK

[ 118 ]

## MAP III

### NATIVE TREES FOUND IN THE ASILOMAR BEACH STATE PARK TO PFEIFFER— BIG SUR STATE PARK AREA

(1) Monterey Pine      Coast Live Oak
     Monterey Cypress      Wax Myrtle

(2) Bishop Pine

(3) Madrone (a single tree)

(4) Black Cottonwood      Monterey Pine
     Arroyo Willow      Monterey Cypress
     Box Elder      Western Sycamore

(5) Gowan Cypress      Monterey Cypress
     Monterey Pine      Toyon
     Coast Live Oak

(6) Red Alder      Golden Willow
     California Laurel      Arroyo Willow
     Big Leaf Maple      Coast Live Oak
     Coast Redwood      Madrone (rare)
     Tanbark Oak      California Buckeye
     Red Willow

(7) Santa Lucia Fir      Coast Live Oak
     Coulter Pine      Canyon Live Oak
     Western Yellow Pine      Oracle Oak
     Monterey Pine      California Walnut
     Coast Redwood      Western Sycamore
     Monterey Cypress      California Laurel
     Incense Cedar      Big Leaf Maple
     Black Cottonwood      California Buckeye
     Arroyo Willow      Madrone
     White Alder      Blue Elderberry
     Golden Chinquapin      Wax Myrtle
     Tanbark Oak

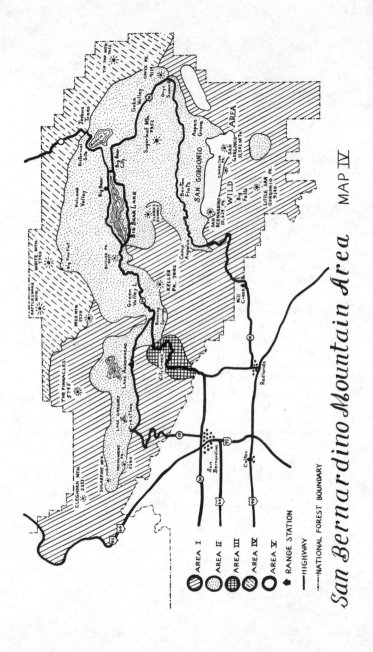

*San Bernardino Mountain Area*  MAP Ⅳ

○ AREA Ⅰ
○ AREA Ⅱ
○ AREA Ⅲ
○ AREA Ⅳ
○ AREA Ⅴ

◆ RANGE STATION
—— HIGHWAY
------ NATIONAL FOREST BOUNDARY

MAP IV

## NATIVE TREES FOUND IN THE
## SAN BERNARDINO MOUNTAIN AREA:

Much of the terrain in this area is abruptly varied and rugged, producing a rapid succession of changing plant environments. Hence, in general, the various trees will be located by areas rather than by specific spot locations. Individual species will frequently be widely scattered within a specified area. However, a significant number of the trees listed for areas I and II will be found along Highway 38 from Mill Creek Ranger Station to Big Bear City and environs. Likewise, many of the trees listed for area III will be found along Highway 30 from the National Forest boundary to Running Spring and environs. Cases of overlap will be found along area boundaries. No claim is made for a complete listing within each area.

### AREA I

| | |
|---|---|
| Coulter Pine | Mountain Mahogany |
| Big Cone Spruce | Fremont Cottonwood |
| Coast Live Oak | Black Cottonwood |
| Canyon Live Oak | Western Sycamore |
| White Alder | |

### AREA II

| | |
|---|---|
| Western Yellow Pine | California Black Oak |
| Jeffrey Pine | Fremont Cottonwood |
| Sugar Pine | Black Cottonwood |
| Coulter Pine | Aspen |
| Lodgepole Pine | Red Willow |
| One Leaf Piñon Pine | Yellow Willow |
| Incense Cedar | Nuttall Willow |
| White Fir | Arroyo Willow |
| Western Juniper | White Alder |
| Big Cone Spruce | Western Sycamore |
| Canyon Live Oak | Bigberry Manzanita |

| | |
|---|---|
| Mountain Mahogany | Big Leaf Maple |
| Mountain Dogwood | Mountain Maple |
| Blue Elderberry | Bitter Cherry |
| Toyon | Western Choke Cherry |
| Box Elder | |

## AREA III

| | |
|---|---|
| Coulter Pine | California Black Oak |
| Knobcone Pine | Canyon Live Oak |
| Sugar Pine | Interior Live Oak |
| Jeffrey Pine | Bigberry Manzanita |
| Big Cone Spruce | Black Cottonwood |
| Toyon | Western Sycamore |

## AREA IV

| | |
|---|---|
| Coulter Pine | Red Willow |
| One Leaf Piñon Pine | Fremont Cottonwood |
| California Juniper | Western Sycamore |
| Canyon Live Oak | White Alder |
| Interior Live Oak | Joshua Tree |

## AREA V and VA

| | |
|---|---|
| Limber Pine | Sugar Pine |
| Lodgepole Pine | Black Cottonwood |
| Aspen | Bigberry Manzanita |
| Incense Cedar | Western Juniper VA |
| Jeffrey Pine | One Leaf Piñon Pine VA |

### PRIVATELY ENDOWED BOTANIC GARDENS

We are fortunate in southern California to have two excellent privately endowed and supported botanic gardens devoted to the propagation and study of native and hybridized California plants. Both gardens are open to the public. The Rancho Santa Ana Botanic Garden was founded in 1927 by Susanna Bixby Bryant in the rolling foothills in the Santa Ana Canyon area. In 1948 it was relocated on an eighty-acre site at 1500 North College Avenue in Claremont about a third of a mile north of Foothill Boulevard (U. S. Highway 66). Except for some magnificent Coast Live Oaks most of the trees in the garden have been planted since 1948, hence they exhibit for the most part the characteristics of the immature tree. However, many specimens do display the major features which these species assume in a semi-protected environment. Seventy-nine of the ninety trees described in this volume are found in the garden. In addition to native trees, the garden has an extensive collection of shrubs, herbs, desert, and seashore plants, as well as a home demonstration garden showing the landscape use of native plants.

The Santa Barbara Botanic Garden, located at 1212 Mission Canyon Road in Santa Barbara, was established in 1926 at the instigation of a small group of citizens interested in the preservation and study of the native flora of California. Mrs. Anna Blaksley Bliss purchased the first fifteen acres in the memory of her father, Henry J. Blaksley, for whom the garden was originally named. More land has been added from time to time so that it now contains fifty acres. In 1939 the name was changed to Santa Barbara Botanic Garden. Most of the trees found in the garden are quite mature and exhibit in general the characteristics shown by these specimens when they are grown in a somewhat protected environment. Sixty-eight native trees of Southern California are found in this well-designed and interesting garden. It also contains an extensive collection of shrubs, herbs, and other plants. Special attention has been focused on the use of native plants in home gardens. The spring flower display is spectacular in both of these gardens. A visit to either or both of these gardens will be profitable and enjoyable. Their directors and supporters are to be commended for their outstanding contributions. See check list, page 134, for the native trees of southern California which are to be found in these gardens.

## ACTIVITIES

### Make an Area Tree Map

When you travel about the state, either by road or trail, secure or make a map of the area. Name and locate on it the various species of trees that you see. Take silhouette pictures of a typical specimen of each species, and, if possible, take colored pictures of its fruit, leaves, and bark. File these with the map for future review and reference.

### Make a Herbarium

You may wish to make a herbarium including the species which you have identified and located on your tree map. If so, collect typical leaves, flowers (if available), fruit, twigs showing buds (if possible), and bark. Place the leaves, flowers, and twigs between heavy layers of newspapers or blotters to dry, being careful to place specimens so that they do not overlap each other. Several separate specimen-containing layers

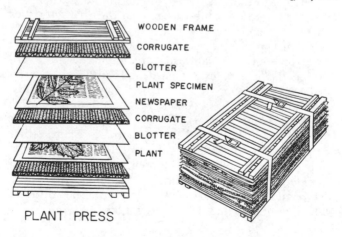

WOODEN FRAME
CORRUGATE
BLOTTER
PLANT SPECIMEN
NEWSPAPER
CORRUGATE
BLOTTER
PLANT

PLANT PRESS

may be laid on top of each other and the entire package placed between two pieces of uniformly weighted plywood or heavy cardboard. (If you plan an extensive herbarium you may wish to make or buy a herbarium press.) When specimens are thoroughly dry they should be mounted with special tape or a special glue on heavy stiff paper on which should be noted the name of the species, location, and date of collection.

HERBARIUM SHEET

Each paper should be filed separately in a manila folder and stored in a closed container. Large cones, when properly labeled, may be kept on shelves or in open containers. Small cones, acorns, bark, and some small dried fruits may be conveniently stored and displayed in discarded cellophane-topped Christmas card boxes. In some cases you may wish to place the specimens on a pad of cotton in order to hold them in place and near the top of the container.

Permanently mounted specimens which have been correctly identified will prove very helpful in identifying new material.

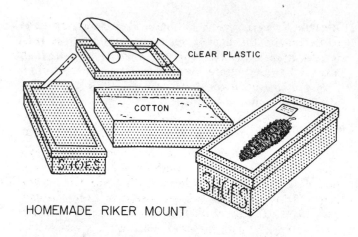

CLEAR PLASTIC

COTTON

SHOES

SHOES

HOMEMADE RIKER MOUNT

## Make a Check List of Local Native Trees

Make a check list of the native trees found in your community. Indicate on a map the specific location of each species. Which of these trees was planted by man? Compare the growth pattern of native trees planted in public parks and home ground with those of the same species found in their native habitat. Account for the variations which you may observe. You may wish to take silhouette pictures and also to make a herbarium collection of specimens from native cultivated trees for comparative purposes.

## Age of Trees

Examine the cross-section of a log cut from near the base of the tree and note the concentric rings which start at or near the center and extend to the perimeter of the log. Each ring represents the growth of one year. Smooth the cut surface with sandpaper and carefully count the rings to determine the age of the tree. You may need a hand lens or a powerful reading glass in order to make an accurate count. Often the stump of an old tree shows the rings quite distinctly. If so, smooth the surface and make a count.

Recount to verify your estimate. Tree rings are used to determine the age of such very old trees as redwoods, cypresses, and junipers. Slender core borings are used to determine the age of standing trees. The size and character of tree rings tell us a great deal about past climatic conditions.

### MAKE AND STUDY A WOOD COLLECTION

Contact some of the lumber companies in your neighborhood to see if you can secure from or through them display samples of woods representing the various native trees of southern California. Unless the samples have already been prepared for display, smooth all surfaces with fine sandpaper and examine each carefully with a hand lens, noting similarities and differences in both surface and end-grain patterns. You will note that no two woods present the same grain patterns. End-grain patterns are very distinctive and provide a positive means of wood identification. Study each sample carefully until you can recognize the same wood when found in a piece of furniture or in a building which is under construction. You may wish to extend your observations to include all of the common commercial woods, irrespective of their source. Make a list of the woods commonly used in furniture and house construction.

### ENEMIES OF OUR FORESTS

Fire, insects, and disease are common enemies of the forest. Which of these account for the greatest financial losses? (Check your estimates with government statistics.) What methods are being used to combat the ravages of each and with what success? What secondary damages occur as a result of each?

### WOOD PRODUCTS

Prepare a list of products derived directly or indirectly from trees. Check your library and various commercial publications for source material. List some products which twenty years ago were derived almost exclusively from trees which are now derived principally from other sources. Account for this change.

## MAKE A LAND UTILIZATION STUDY

Make a study of the land utilization of the United States, noting the following percentage of the national land mass in each of the following categories: 1. forests, (a) public, (b) private: 2. agriculture, (a) cultivation, (b) grazing; 3. non-productive, (a) deserts, (b) barren mountains, (c) swamps and submerged areas. You may wish to study further the type of products produced in the various public and private forests, the extent and success of reforestation, and recovery of non-productive lands through irrigation and drainage. You may wish to record your findings on a map.

## LIFE IN FOREST ENVIRONS

Select a deep forest as a starting point. Note the size and type of trees; the undergrowth, including the smaller annuals; and the animals which inhabit the area. This latter should include the birds, mammals, reptiles, amphibia, and insects. Now proceed towards the edge of the forest and finally into the open meadow. Note the changes in the plant and animal life as you move from one environment to another. Try to account for these changes. This project will take several days since you will need to spend at least an entire day in each of the different areas and some time for re-checking. Why do you suppose that the animals distribute themselves as they do? Why are the leaves of certain plants larger in the forest than in the open meadow? Why do the trees develop a different silhouette in the deep forest than in the open areas? These and dozens of other questions will come to mind as you work with this project, which you may wish to combine with a summer camp trip.

## Study Forest Recovery in Devastated Areas

Select several forest areas for study. In order to have a good basis for comparison you will need to examine some areas which were burned fifteen or twenty years ago and compare these with areas which have been burned recently. List in order of appearance the type of vegetation, including brush and trees, that follows a devastating fire in an open forest and in a dense forest. Note the change in animal habitation in such areas. Note the erosion effects in a denuded area. What are some of the more remote effects of such a catastrophe? List cautions which must be observed to prevent destructive forest fires. What measures can be taken to hasten restoration and to minimize erosion in burned areas?

## Make a Survey of the California Public Recreational Facilities

Secure from the various local, state, and federal agencies maps showing the location of such recreational areas under their jurisdiction as community, city, county, and state parks and beaches and national parks, monuments, and forests. You may wish to locate those areas which lie within southern California on a single map. You will be impressed with the number and extent of publicly owned and controlled reserves. Visit as many of these areas as possible and make notes concerning the following: (*a*) factors which caused the area to be set aside as a public reserve; (*b*) species of native trees found within the area (were they a factor in its selection?); (*c*) provisions being made to protect the longevity of the trees and its effectiveness; (*d*) special provisions that have been made to encourage public use of the area (are these facilities in keeping with good conservation practices?); (*e*) extent to which these areas are being used.

What additional areas in southern California would you propose to be included in any of the above categories? Discuss your proposals with as many interested people as possible. If your proposal appears to have strong general acceptance, contact the proper authorities and attempt to convince them of the merits of your proposal. As the population of southern California continues to grow we will need to greatly expand available and well-manned recreational facilities and especially those in which trees are a factor.

## PROTECTIVE INFLUENCE OF TREES

Trees have, since early times, been used by man as a medium for protection against the adverse effect of such natural elements as heat, cold, wind, rain, and snow. Describe as many situations as you can to illustrate how trees may have been used for these purposes. The habitat of many animals is predicated on the presence of either scattered or forest trees. Name some animals that fall in this category and describe just how they are dependent on trees for food or protection or both. Trees are also an important factor in stabilizing land surfaces. Make a list, based on observation, of the various ways in which trees have been effective in this respect.

Many additional interesting and worthwhile tree activities are described by Woodbridge Metcalf in *Native Trees of the San Francisco Bay Region,* University of California Press.

# SUGGESTED REFERENCES

Munz, Philip and David D. Keck, *A California Flora*. Berkeley: University of California Press, 1959.

McMinn, Howard E. and Evelyn Maino. *An Illustrated Manual of California Trees*. Berkeley: University of California Press, 1947.

Sudworth, George B. *Forest Trees of the Pacific Slope*. Washington, D.C. U.S. Government Printing Office, 1908.

Jepson, Willis Lynn. *Trees of California*. Berkeley Associated Students Store, 1923.

Peattie, Donald C. *A Natural History of Western Trees*. Boston: Houghton Mifflin, 1953.

Metcalf, Woodbridge W. *Native Trees of the San Francisco Bay Region*. Berkeley: University of California Press, 1959.

Watts, Tom. *California Tree Finder*. Berkeley Nature Study Guild. P. O. Box 972, Berkeley, California, 1963.

# GLOSSARY

*anther,* the sac or sacs containing the pollen, the essential part of the stamen.

*appressed,* flattened or pressed against another body but not united with it; hairs lying flat on leaves are appressed.

*axillary,* borne or occurring in an axil.

*axils,* the angle between a leaf and stem.

*bract,* the modified or much reduced leaf of a flower-cluster; in Gramineae, the modified leaf subtending a spikelet; leafy-bracted, in Compositae, with accessory or foliose bracts to the head outside the involucre.

*calyx,* the outer, usually green, whorl of the flower.

*coalesced,* organs of one kind that have grown together.

*constricted,* tightened or drawn together.

*dorsal,* relating to or borne along the back; lower; outer; posterior.

*drupe,* a fruit with a fleshy or soft outside (or exocarp) and a hard or stony inside (or endocarp.)

*filaments,* a thread, in case of a stamen the stalk supporting the anther.

*glabrous,* bald, not hairy. Some agriculturists and some botanists wrongly use the term smooth as opposite to hairy; bald or balbrous is the opposite of hairy; smooth is the opposite of rough.

*glaucous,* whitened with a bloom.

*globose,* rounded, more or less spherical.

*keel,* a longitudinal central ridge on the back of an organ, like the keel of a boat; the two lower petals of a pea-like flower which are joined into a keel-like body.

*midrib,* the main or central rib of a leaf.

*obovate,* inversely ovate.

*petioles,* the stalk of a leaf.

*pinnae,* leaflets or divisions of a compound leaf.

*pubescent,* clothed with hairs, especially soft or downy hairs.

*raceme,* a flower cluster in which the flowers are borne along the peduncle on pedicels of nearly equal length.

*ranked,* successive rows.

*samara,* an indehiscent winged fruit like the key of a maple.

*sessile,* leaf, leaf without a petiole and the blade seated directly on the stem; sessile ovary, one without a stipe.

*spike,* a flower cluster in which the flowers are sessile and more or less densely arranged along a common peduncle.

*spurs,* a slender and hollow extension or prolongation of some part of a flower, as the petal of a Columbine or calyx of a Larkspur.

*stigma,* the receptive part of the style which secretes a sticky or viscid substance.

*stipules,* small supplementary organs or appendages of the leaf, borne in pairs at the base of the petiole.

*stomates,* a breathing pore or aperture in the epidermis.

*style,* the contracted or slender portion of a pistil between the ovary and stigma.

*umbellate,* borne in an umbel.

*ventral,* relating to or borne on the face; upper; inner; anterior.

## CHECK LIST OF SCIENTIFIC AND COMMON NAMES
## OF NATIVE TREES OF SOUTHERN CALIFORNIA

‡* *Pinus monophylla* (One Leaf Piñon Pine), p. 29

‡ *Pinus murrayana* (Lodgepole Pine or Tamarack Pine), p. 31, pl. 1

‡* *Pinus muricata* (Bishop Pine), p. 31, pl. 1

 * *Pinus remorata* (Santa Cruz Island Pine), p. 32, pl. 2

 *Pinus edulis* (Nut Pine), p. 32

‡* *Pinus ponderosa* (Western Yellow Pine or Ponderosa Pine), p. 33, pl. 1

 * *Pinus jeffreyi* (Jeffrey Pine), p. 34, pl. 1

 * *Pinus sabiniana* (Digger Pine), p. 35, pl. 3

 * *Pinus coulteri* (Coulter Pine), p. 35, pl. 3

 * *Pinus radiata* (Monterey Pine), p. 36, pl. 3

 * *Pinus attenuata* (Knobcone Pine), p. 36, pl. 3

 * *Pinus quadrifolia* (Parry Pine), p. 37

 *Pinus lambertiana* (Sugar Pine), p. 39, pl. 4

 *Pinus aristata* (Bristlecone Pine), p. 40, pl. 4

 *Pinus flexilis* (Limber Pine), p. 40

‡* *Pinus torreyana* (Torrey Pine), p. 41

‡* *Pseudotsuga menziesii* (Douglas Fir), p. 42, pl. 4

‡* *Pseudotsuga macrocarpa* (Big Cone Spruce), p. 43, pl. 4

‡* *Abies concolor* (White Fir), p. 44, pl. 5

‡* *Abies bracteata* (Santa Lucia Fir or Bristlecone Fir), p. 44

‡* *Sequoia sempervirens* (Coast Redwood), p. 46, pl. 5

‡* *Callo decurrens* (Incense Cedar), p. 47, pl. 5

‡* *Cupressus macrocarpa* (Monterey Cypress), p. 48

 * *Cupressus goveniana* (Gowan Cypress), p. 49, pl. 5

 * *Cupressus stephensonii* (Cuyamaca Cypress), p. 49 pl. 6

‡* *Cupressus forbesii* (Tecate Cypress), p. 50, pl. 6

‡* *Cupressus sargentii* (Sargent Cypress), p. 50

‡* *Juniperus occidentalis* (Western Juniper), p. 51

‡* *Juniperus californica* (California Juniper), p. 52

‡* *Juniperus osteosperma* (Utah Juniper), p. 52. pl. 6

‡* *Washingtonia filifera* (California Fan Palm or Desert Palm), p. 55

‡* *Yucca brevifolia* (Joshua Tree), p. 56, pl. 7

 * *Yucca schidigera* (Mojave Yucca or Spanish Dagger), p. 57, pl. 7

‡* *Myrica californica* (Wax Myrtle), p. 59

\* *Can be seen in Santa Barbara Botanic Garden*
‡ *Can be seen in Rancho Santa Ana Botanic Garden*

[ 134 ]

| | |
|---|---|
| * *Juglans californica* | (California Walnut), p. 59 |
| *Populus tremuloides* | (Aspen or Quaking Aspen), p. 61 |
| ‡* *Populus fremontii* | (Fremont Cottonwood), p. 62 |
| ‡* *Populus trichocarpa* | (Black Cottonwood), p. 63, pl.6 |
| * *Salix laevigata* | (Red Willow), p. 64, pl. 8 |
| * *Salix lasiandra* | (Golden Willow), p. 64, pl. 8 |
| *Salix gooddingii* | (Black Willow), p. 65, pl. 8 |
| ‡* *Salix lasiolepis* | (Arroyo Willow), p. 65, pl. 8 |
| *Salix scouleriana* | (Nuttall Willow), p. 66 pl. 9 |
| *Salix lutea* var. *watsonii* | (Watson's Willow), p. 66 |
| * *Salix hindsiana* | (Sandbar Willow, Valley Willow, or Gray Narrow Leaf Willow), p. 66 pl. 9 |
| ‡* *Alnus rhombifolia* | (White Alder), p. 67 |
| ‡ *Alnus oregona* | (Red Alder), p. 68, pl. 9 |
| ‡ *Castanopsis chrysophylla* var. *minor* | (Golden Chinquapin), p .70 |
| ‡* *Lithocarpus densiflora* | (Tanbark Oak), p. 70, pl. 9 |
| ‡* *Quercus lobata* | (Valley Oak), p. 72, pl. 10 |
| ‡* *Quercus douglasii* | (Blue Oak), p. 72, pl. 11 |
| ‡ *Quercus engelmannii* | (Engelmann Oak), p. 73, pl. 11 |
| ‡* *Quercus chrysolepis* | (Canyon Live Oak, Maul Oak, Gold Cup Oak, or Iron Oak), p. 73, pl. 11 |
| ‡* *Quercus agrifolia* | (Coast Live Oak or California Live Oak), p. 74, pl. 11 |
| ‡* *Quercus wislizenii* | (Interior Live Oak), p. 75, pl. 12 |
| ‡* *Quercus kelloggii* | (California Black Oak), p. 75, pl. 12 |
| ‡ *Quercus morehus* | (Oracle Oak), p. 76, pl. 12 |
| ‡* *Quercus palmeri* | (Palmer Oak), p. 76, pl. 12 |
| ‡* *Umbellularia californica* | (California Laurel, Oregon Myrtle, Bay Laurel, California Bay, or Pepperwood), p. 77, pl. 13 |
| ‡* *Platanus racemosa* | (Sycamore), p. 78 |
| ‡ *Cercocarpus ledifolius* | (Mountain Mahogany or Curlleaf Mahogany), p. 79 |
| ‡* *Cercocarpus betuloides* | (Hard Tack or Birch-leaf Mahogany), p. 80, pl. 13 |
| ‡* *Prunus emarginata* | (Bitter Cherry), p. 80 |
| ‡* *Prunus fremontii* | (Desert Apricot), p. 81, pl. 13 |
| ‡ *Prunus virginiana* | (Western Choke Cherry), p. 82 |